D0670967

ATHENS

ENCOUNTER

VICTORIA KYRIAKOPOULOS

Athens Encounter

Published by Lonely Planet Publications Pty Ltd
ABN 36 005 607 983

Australia	Head Office, Locked Bag 1, Footscray, Victoria 3011 ☎ 03 8379 8000 fax 03 8379 8111 talk2us@lonelyplanet.com.au
USA	150 Linden St, Oakland, CA 94607 ☎ 510 250 6400 toll free 800 275 8555 fax 510 893 8572 info@lonelyplanet.com
UK	2nd fl, 186 City Rd London EC1V 2NT ☎ 020 7106 2100 fax 020 7106 2101 go@lonelyplanet.co.uk

This title was commissioned in Lonely Planet's London office and produced by: **Commissioning Editors** Fiona Buchan, Michala Green, Sally Schafer **Coordinating Editor** Gina Tsarouhas **Coordinating Cartographer** Julie Dodkins **Layout Designer** Jacqui Saunders **Assisting Editors** Monique Choy, Diana Saad **Assisting Cartographers** Valentina Kremenchutskaya, Joanne Luke **Assisting Layout Designer** Jim Hsu, Indra Kilfoyle, Wibowo Rusli **Managing Editor** Geoff Howard **Managing Cartographer** Mark Griffiths **Cover Designer** Tamsin Wilson **Project Managers** Eoin Dunlevy, Fabrice Rocher **Managing Layout Designer** Celia Wood **Thanks to** Shahara Ahmed, Glenn Beanland, David Connolly, Quentin Frayne, Laura Jane, Chris Lee Ack, Charity Mackinnon, Wayne Murphy, Michael Ruff, Julie Sheridan, Geoff Stringer

ISBN 978 1 74104 991 6

Printed by Hang Tai Printing Company
Printed in China.

Acknowledgement Athens Metro Map © 2008 Attiko Metro

HOW TO USE THIS BOOK

Colour-Coding & Maps

Colour-coding is used for symbols on maps and in the text that they relate to (eg all eating venues on the maps and in the text are given a green knife and fork symbol). Each neighbourhood also gets its own colour, and this is used down the edge of the page and throughout that neighbourhood section.

Shaded yellow areas on the maps denote 'areas of interest' – for their historical significance, their attractive architecture or their great bars and restaurants. We encourage you to head to these areas and just start exploring!

Prices

Multiple prices listed with reviews (eg €10/5 or €10/5/20) indicate adult/child, adult/concession or adult/child/family.

Send us your feedback We love to hear from readers – your comments help make our books better. We read every word you send us, and we always guarantee that your feedback goes straight to the appropriate authors. The most useful submissions are rewarded with a free book. To send us your updates and find out about Lonely Planet events, newsletters and travel news visit our award-winning website: *lonelyplanet.com/contact*.

Note: We may edit, reproduce and incorporate your comments in Lonely Planet products such as guidebooks, websites and digital products, so let us know if you don't want your comments reproduced or your name acknowledged. For a copy of our privacy policy visit *lonelyplanet.com/privacy*.

VICTORIA KYRIAKOPOULOS

Victoria left her hometown, Melbourne, for a year-long Athens experiment in 2000 and ended up staying four years – and the city still feels like home whenever she returns. Since her very first visit in 1988, she's witnessed Athens' remarkable transformation. Despite its quirks and frustrations, she's never ceased to be captivated by Athens' heady jumble of history, urban life, restless energy and hedonistic spirit. She was editor of the Athens-based Greek diaspora magazine *Odyssey*, reported on the city's Olympics preparations for the *Age* and various Australian and international newspapers and magazines, and worked on several TV shows about Greece. She wrote the previous editions of *Best of Athens*, the Athens chapter of *Greece* 8 and the last two editions of *Crete*. When not living her 'other' life in Greece, she is a freelance journalist based in Melbourne.

VICTORIA'S THANKS

Special thanks to Eleni Bertes for her invaluable support. For their help, insight and company, thanks to Antonis Bekiaris, Eleni Gialama, Kamilo Nollas, Mary Retiniotis, Spiros Nasainas, Vasilis Zenios, Maria Zygourakis, Nikos Dimopoulos, Eleni Hatziladas and Tammy Iliou. In Melbourne, thanks to Bill and Yvonne Kyriakopoulos, Rosanna De Marco and Chris Anastassiades; in London thanks to Sally Schafer and Michala Green at Lonely Planet.

THE PHOTOGRAPHER

George Tsafos has been a contributor to Lonely Planet Images for almost nine years. George took up travel photography almost 13 years ago while he was searching for a good way to escape the daily routine. Born and raised in Athens, he is currently working freelance for magazines and newspapers both national and international. He's also been a technical editor for almost a decade, writing articles on photography and digital imaging. His first technical book on digital photography was published in 2006.

Cover photograph Exhibits at the National Archaeological Museum, Exarhia, Athens, John Sones/Lonely Planet Images. **Internal photographs** p54, p72, p106, p128 by Victoria Kyriakopoulos; p26, p152 Scott Barbour/Getty Images. All other photographs by Lonely Planet Images, and by George Tsafos except p24, p29, p98, p105, p107 Anders Blomqvist; p100, p135, p141 Neil Setchfield; p147 Diana Mayfield; p150 Holger Leue.
All images are copyright of the photographers unless otherwise indicated. Many of the images in this guide are available for licensing from **Lonely Planet Images:** www.lonelyplanetimages.com.

Patrons enjoying a drink at the charming bar Alier Man (p92), Gazi

CONTENTS

Why is our travel information the best in the world? It's simple: our authors are passionate, dedicated travellers. They don't take freebies in exchange for positive coverage so you can be sure the advice you're given is impartial. They travel widely to all the popular spots, and off the beaten track. They don't research using just the internet or phone. They discover new places not included in any other guidebook. They personally visit thousands of hotels, restaurants, palaces, trails, galleries, temples and more. They speak with dozens of locals every day to make sure you get the kind of insider knowledge only a local could tell you. They take pride in getting all the details right, and in telling it how it is. Think you can do it? Find out how at **lonelyplanet.com**.

V

THIS IS ATHENS

THIS IS ATHENS

From the iconic Acropolis rising majestically above the city to modish galleries and lively bars in gritty downtown backstreets, bustling Athens is a delightfully quirky clash of past and present, a city that confronts and surprises.

Major urban renewal has breathed new life into Athens' historic centre, spectacularly reconciling its ancient and modern faces with charming car-free streets that wind along well-trodden ancient paths, making it feel like you're walking through a giant archaeological park. Ancient monuments bask in the famous Attica light that softens the concrete sprawl.

Amongst the downtown hurly-burly and traffic-ridden roads, you'll find quiet shaded cafés and delightful neighbourhood squares, sophisticated shopping strips, quaint tavernas and chic restaurants. Amid the sea of modern high-rise office and apartment blocks you'll find Byzantine churches, restored neoclassical buildings and equal measures of grunge and grace.

While Athens' wealth of archaeological sites and museums remains its drawcard, it's the city's vibe and mindset that enamours and surprises visitors. An infectious, restless energy permeates this city; pavements bustle with Athenians revelling in the lively alfresco café and dining cultures, while balmy summer nights have a seductive allure. Vibrant street life creates a chaotic yet almost permanently festive atmosphere.

Athens comes alive at twilight and stays up late – its spirited nightlife sustains arguably more bars and clubs than many other world capitals. Athens continues to be a city of change. The city's radical pre-Olympics makeover went well beyond new infrastructure. There's a newfound confidence and creative energy, particularly in emerging arts, dining and entertainment hotspots in newly hip, urban neighbourhoods. Yet despite its urbane ambitions, Athens retains a distinctly east-meets-west character; at the same time folksy and sophisticated, traditional and anarchic, frenetic and laid-back, often frustrating but inevitably fun.

Top left Strolling through the ancient cemetery ruins of Keramikos (p22) **Top right** Relaxing at a café on the Ancient Promenade (p13) with the Acropolis (p10) as a backdrop **Bottom** The Caryatids standing sentinel at the iconic Erechtheion (p10)

ATHENS >7

The illuminated Temple of Hephaestus (p62) seen at dusk from the rooftop restaurant of Kuzina (p83)

>1 ACROPOLIS

MARVEL AT THE ZENITH OF CLASSICAL CIVILISATION

The greatest symbol of the glory of ancient Greece – the magnificent Parthenon – rises spectacularly over Athens. The temple is built on the highest point of the Acropolis (High City), the ancient city of temples on the sacred rocky plateau that dominates the city.

Inhabited since neolithic times, the Acropolis has been a place of cult worship, a fortress, and it once had a Mycenaean palace on the peak. Early temples dedicated to the goddess Athena were destroyed by the Persians in 480 BC. During Athens' golden age, Pericles transformed the Acropolis into a magnificent city of temples that has come to be regarded as the high point of classical Greek achievement.

The centrepiece was the Parthenon, the largest Doric temple ever completed in Greece, finished in time for the Great Panathenaic Festival of 438 BC. The soaring marble columns were ingeniously curved to create an optical illusion of a harmonious, perfect form. Brightly coloured and gilded sculptured friezes (the controversial Parthenon marbles in the British Museum) depicted various battles of the times and the Panathenaic procession. The Parthenon housed the colossal 10m-high gold and ivory statue of Athena – created by the famous sculptor Pheidias – and served as the treasury for the Delian League.

Under successive occupiers, the temples on the Acropolis were converted into churches, mosques and military strongholds. The biggest catastrophe came in 1687 when the Venetians opened fire on the ruling Turks, who stored gunpowder in the Parthenon, causing a massive explosion that severely damaged the temples.

At the entrance to the Acropolis is the 3rd-century Beulé Gate and beyond it the Propylaia, the monumental entrance to the city – the entrance had a gate leading to the Panathenaic Way, the route taken by the Panathenaic procession.

On the southwestern edge, the elegant small Temple of Athena Nike, originally built by Callicrates (c 420 BC), is being painstakingly reconstructed after being removed entirely for restoration in 2002.

The iconic Erechtheion, with its six-column maidens known as the Caryatids, stands on the Acropolis' most sacred spot, where, in a contest for the city, Poseidon struck the ground with his trident producing a

spring of water and Athena in turn produced the olive tree (she won).
Four of the original columns are in the new Acropolis Museum.

Time, war, pilfering, earthquakes, pollution and botched restoration efforts have taken their toll on the Acropolis. Cranes and scaffolding have been virtually permanent fixtures since massive conservation efforts began in 1975.

The old on-site museum will exhibit historic photos and priceless sketches and paintings of old Athens by foreign travellers.

See also p52 for details.

>2 ACROPOLIS MUSEUM
ADMIRE THE MARBLE TREASURES OF THE ACROPOLIS

Athens' long-awaited new Acropolis Museum is at the southern foot of the Acropolis. Priceless sculptures and reliefs were carefully transferred from the small on-site former museum to their new €130-million state-of-the-art home, bringing together more than 4000 artefacts, many of which were in storage or other museums.

Natural light masterfully re-creates outdoor conditions; massive columns evoke the temples; and the design allows exhibits to be viewed from several vantage points. A glass ramp symbolising the ascent to the Acropolis leads to the Archaic gallery, a virtual forest of sculptures. Four Caryatids take pride of place on the 2nd level, where the restaurant enjoys spectacular views. The top-floor glass atrium presents a mirror image of the 161m-long frieze that ran around the Parthenon, for the first time setting it in context. Clearly differentiated casts of the missing pieces – the British Museum houses about 75m of the frieze – make a convincing argument for their return. The Parthenon's stunning triangular pedimental sculptures stand at each end, while the metopes are placed relatively in situ – all within sight of the sacred rock.

The museum stands on pylons, with glass floors exposing the expansive ruins of an ancient Athenian neighbourhood uncovered during excavation works.

See also p52.

>3 ANCIENT PROMENADE

STROLL AROUND THE HEART OF ANCIENT AND MODERN ATHENS

A grand pedestrian promenade connecting the city's most significant ancient sites has radically transformed Athens' historic centre.
The delightful, traffic-free 3km promenade – reputedly Europe's
longest pedestrian precinct – has reconciled ancient and modern
Athens and made it a focal point of Athens' vibrant street life. In
the evenings, locals and tourists alike delight in a leisurely *volta*
(stroll) along the wide cobblestone boulevard that winds around the
foothills of the floodlit Acropolis. Open-air art exhibitions, book fairs,
buskers, street traders and vendors add to the festive atmosphere.

Starting at Dionysiou Areopagitou, opposite the Temple of
Olympian Zeus (p43), the walkway takes you along the southern
foothills of the Acropolis (p52), past the Odeon of Herodes Atticus
(p57) to Filopappou Hill, then along Apostolou Pavlou past an
open-air cinema, Thission (p87), Socrates Prison (Map pp78–9, D6)
and Thisio's bustling cafés (p82) to the Ancient Agora (p62). Near
Thisio metro, it branches west to Keramikos (p80) and Gazi (p88)
and veers north through Monastiraki to the atmospheric streets of
Plaka (p58).

>4 NATIONAL ARCHAEOLOGICAL MUSEUM

DISCOVER THE SPLENDOUR OF GREECE'S ANTIQUITIES

Greece's pre-eminent museum houses the world's largest and finest collection of Greek antiquities and should not be missed. The museum's treasures date back to the neolithic era (6800 BC) and include items from the Bronze Age and the Cycladic, Minoan, Mycenaean and classical periods, with exquisite pottery and frescoes, jewellery and countless other artefacts found throughout Greece. Housed in an imposing neoclassical building since late 1800s, the refurbished museum reopened all its galleries in 2008 (some had been closed since damage sustained in the 1999 earthquake).

Highlights are grouped on the 1st floor in the prehistoric collection, including the fabulous collection of Mycenaean antiquities. The exquisite gold treasures, found in unlooted tombs excavated by Heinrich Schliemann at Mycenae in the 1800s, include the celebrated 1600 BC funerary mask of Agamemnon and the Vaphio cups. The Cycladic collection (Gallery 6), from the civilisation that flourished in the Bronze Age on the Cycladic islands, includes the superb iconic figurines that inspired artists such as Picasso.

The development of Greek sculpture is displayed in the superb eponymous collection, whose highlights include the colossal 3m-high marble Sounion Kouros (600 BC; Gallery 8) found at the Temple of Poseidon, the 460 BC bronze statue of Zeus or Poseidon (no one really knows which) holding a thunderbolt or trident (Gallery 15) and the striking 2nd-century BC statue of a horse and young rider (Gallery 21), recovered from a shipwreck.

Another crowd-pleaser is the Thira gallery, displaying the spectacular Minoan frescoes uncovered in Akrotiri, on Santorini, after being buried in a volcanic eruption in the 16th century.

The excellent pottery collection traces its development from the Bronze Age, including the famous Attic black-figured pottery and the uniquely Athenian slender Attic white Lekythoi vases depicting scenes at tombs.

The Stathatos gallery, bequeathed in the 1950s, has to-die-for jewellery, small figurines, vases and objects from various period. Reopened in 2008, the two-room Egyptian gallery presents the best of the museum's 7000-strong collection, considered one of world's finest. Spanning more than 3000 years from the pre-dynastic period to Roman times, the gallery includes mummies, Fayum portraits and a prized bronze figurine of princess Takushit.

See also p104.

>5 PLAKA

EXPLORE ATHENS' ATMOSPHERIC OLD QUARTER

Plaka, the historic neighbourhood under the Acropolis, has long
been a magnet for travellers and Athenians alike. Touristy in the
extreme, it is undeniably atmospheric and charming, especially if
you venture beyond the busy drag of souvenir stores and tavernas.
Plaka's stone-paved narrow streets give you a palpable sense of
history, with ancient monuments and streets such as Adrianou and
Tripodon that follow the paths of ancient roads, Byzantine churches,
and eclectic small museums in restored neoclassical mansions.

Much of Plaka is the old Turkish quarter that was virtually all that
existed when Athens was declared capital of independent Greece,
though few Ottoman structures survive. Gentrification has made teh
area one of Athens' more exclusive neighbourhoods, though it has
its share of crumbling buildings.

Directly under the Acropolis is the delightful Anafiotika quarter, a picturesque labyrinth of quiet, narrow, winding paths with
whitewashed island-style houses decorated with bougainvillea and
colourful flower pots. They were built by stonemasons from the
island of Anafi, who came to build the king's palace during the building boom after Independence.

See also p58.

>6 ANCIENT AGORA
FOLLOW THE FOOTSTEPS OF SOCRATES

Greece's best-preserved *agora* (market, or place of assembly) gives invaluable insight into the workings of ancient Athens. It was the bustling hub of civic life, government and social and commercial activity, housing the law courts and the market. Socrates came here to expound his philosophy, and in AD 49 St Paul came to win converts to Christianity. The Ancient Agora was rebuilt in the 5th century BC after being destroyed by the Persians in 480 BC and flourished until AD 267.

The Agora Museum is housed in the restored Stoa of Attalos (138 BC), essentially a 45-column, two-storey elite shopping arcade and hangout for rich Athenians. The museum has a significant collection of finds, including a 5th-century terracotta water clock used to time speeches.

More than 400 modern buildings were demolished to uncover the Ancient Agora during excavations in the 1950s. The 11th-century Church of the Holy Apostles of Solakis, which has some fine Byzantine frescoes, was preserved.

The site has many significant ruins and building foundations but the most impressive is the 449 BC Temple of Hephaestus (also known as the Thisseion) at the western end, the best-preserved Doric temple in Greece. Dedicated to the god of metallurgy, the frieze on the eastern side depicts nine of the 12 labours of Heracles.

See also p62.

>7 ATHENS BY THE SEA

GET INTO THE SUMMER GROOVE AT ATHENS' BEACHES

During Athens' long, hot summers, much of the city's social and cultural life shifts to the seaside. Athenians flock to the crowded beaches, stroll along the waterfront in the evenings and party at chic beach bars and massive summer nightclubs until dawn.

The coastline stretches about 25km south along the Saronic Gulf. The seafront is lined with restaurants, bars and cafés, children's playgrounds, a go-cart track, marinas and an open-air cinema. A scenic tram line from Syntagma runs south along Leoforos Posidonos to Voula, while a second route veers north to the sports stadiums near Piraeus.

Ongoing waterfront redevelopment along the coastline has dramatically improved beachside Athens, from the flashy new Flisvos mega-yacht marina to the former Olympics venues now used for concerts and cultural events.

While there are free public beaches scattered along the coast, most of the better ones have entrance fees but include excellent facilities.

Glyfada marks the beginning of a stretch of coastline known as the Apollo Coast, which has a string of fine beaches running south to Cape Sounion.

See also p142.

>8 ATHENS FROM ABOVE

HEAD TO THE HILLS FOR COOL BREEZES AND STUNNING VISTAS

The pine- and cypress-covered hills surrounding Athens are a cool and peaceful respite from the concrete sprawl, with pleasant walking paths and stunning views. Rising dramatically from the sea of apartment blocks, Lykavittos (p111) is the other hill dominating the Athens skyline. A funicular railway takes you through the rock face to the summit and the landmark white Chapel of Agios Georgios, impressively floodlit at night. You can take in the view in style at the Orizontes (p119) restaurant and café. The open-air Lykavittos Theatre, on the northern slope, hosts summer concerts and theatrical performances.

Southwest of the Acropolis, Filopappou Hill (Map pp78–9, D8), also known as the Hill of the Muses, offers the best eye-level views of the Acropolis from the top, where the Monument of Filopappos was built in AD 114–16 in honour of the Roman governor. The 16th-century Church of Agios Dimitrios Loumbardiaris (Greek for cannon), is named after an incident in which a gunner from a Turkish garrison on the Acropolis was killed by thunderbolt while attempting to fire a cannon on the Christian congregation.

North of Filopappou, the smaller and less-visited Hill of the Pnyx was the meeting place of the Democratic Assembly in the 5th century BC, while the nearby Hill of the Nymphs has the 1840s Old Athens Observatory on the summit.

>9 BENAKI MUSEUM
TAKE AN EASY CRASH COURSE IN GREEK HISTORY

One of the country's finest private museums, the Benaki was founded in 1930 by the son of a wealthy Alexandrian merchant in the family's stunning mansion. Representing the spectrum of Greece's historical and cultural development and the Hellenistic world, the collection features Benaki's eclectic acquisitions from Asia and Europe and pieces from the Byzantine and post-Byzantine eras, as well as significant later bequests.

More than 20,000 items are displayed chronologically over four levels, from prehistory to the formation of the modern Greek state. The antiquities collection includes Bronze Age finds from Mycenae and Thessaly and Cycladic pottery, while the Egyptian collection includes Greco-Roman Fayum funerary portraits. Among the relatively more-recent exhibits are *karagiozi* (shadow puppets), costumes, jewellery and textiles, and paintings, including early works by El Greco (aka Domenicos Theotokopoulos).

A fine café-restaurant on the terrace overlooks the National Gardens and there's an excellent gift shop. The Benaki is a key cultural player in Athens. Contemporary exhibitions are held at the impressive Benaki Museum Pireos Annexe (p90), while a dedicated Islamic Art Museum (p80) houses Benaki's extensive Islamic collection.

See also p111.

>10 ODEON OF HERODES ATTICUS

CATCH A SHOW AT THE HISTORIC HERODION UNDER THE ACROPOLIS

An unforgettable Athens experience is a summer's night at the superb Odeon of Herodes Atticus, known as the Herodion, one of the world's most historic and evocative cultural venues. Set against a floodlit Acropolis, patrons sit under the stars on the worn marble seats (cushions provided) that Athenians have been entertained on for centuries (leave the stilettos at home, they damage the marble).

Built by Herodes Atticus in AD 161 in memory of his wife, Regilla, it was one of ancient Athens' last grand public buildings. The arched ruins of an imposing three-storey stage building make a stunning backdrop to the semicircular theatre, which once had a cedar roof over parts of the stage.

Excavated in the 1850s, it was restored in time for the 1955 Athens Festival (p27) and its majestic stage has since been graced by the likes of opera greats from Callas to Pavarotti, ballet legends Nureyev and Fonteyn, and anything from the New York Philharmonic to the Peking Opera.

The theatre remains Athens' premiere, and most inspiring, venue for summer performances of drama, music and dance by leading local and international artists.

The Herodion is the ultimate of Athens' open-air cultural offerings, which range from moonlight cinema to concerts and theatre in outdoor amphitheatres on hilltops, parks and old quarries.

See also p57.

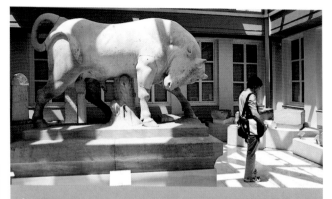

>11 KERAMIKOS

PAYING HOMAGE TO THE ANCIENTS

As well as being the largest and best-preserved classical necropolis, the Keramikos cemetery is a delightful green oasis in downtown Athens, especially in spring when wildflowers are in bloom. Named after the potters' workshops that once thrived in the area, it was the Athenian burial ground from 3000 BC to the 6th century AD. The grand Street of Tombs, where the elite were buried, has some impressive tombs, notably a 4th-century-BC marble bull in the plot of Dionysos of Kollytos. The one in situ is a replica – the original and many other precious finds, including pottery, funerary offerings and toys (including knucklebones), are in the small but excellent on-site museum.

Keramikos is also the site of the once-massive Dipylon Gate, where processions entered the city on their way to the Acropolis (p10) via the Ancient Agora (p17). A hard-to-spot plaque marks the ruins of the gate, but it starts to make sense as you see the Acropolis ahead. You can also see the foundations of the Sacred Gate through which pilgrims took the Sacred Way to Eleusis. Metro excavation works uncovered a wealth of treasures, including more than 7000 *ostraka* – pottery shards inscribed with the names of ostracised Athenian statesmen.

See also p80.

>12 GOULANDRIS MUSEUM OF CYCLADIC & ANCIENT GREEK ART

BEHOLD THE CYCLADIC FIGURES THAT INSPIRED PICASSO

This exceptional private museum houses the biggest independent collection of Cycladic art in the world, as well as an impressive collection of ancient Greek art. Built in 1986 for the Goulandris collection, belonging to one of Greece's richest shipping families, the museum has since expanded into the stunning 19th-century Stathatos mansion and an adjacent wing used for temporary exhibitions.

The Cycladic collection includes life-sized marble statues, tiny figurines and pottery from the civilisation that flourished in the Aegean around the sacred island of Delos from 3200 to 2000 BC. The distinctive, white, minimalist slender figurines of the Cycladic era, depicting raw human forms, have long inspired modern artists and sculptors, including Pablo Picasso, Amedeo Modigliani and Henry Moore. The upper floors house collections from the Mycenaean period to the 14th century (including 8th-century-BC Corinthian bronze helmets and fine terracotta vases), artefacts from the Bronze Age to the Late Roman period and the largest collection of Cypriot antiquities in Greece.

The pleasant atrium café is a great pit stop and the gift shop is well worth a look. See also p114.

>13 BYZANTINE & CHRISTIAN MUSEUM

DELVE INTO THE BYZANTINE WORLD

An outstanding collection of early Christian and Byzantine art is beautifully presented in this fine museum focusing on a significant epoch and part of Greece's cultural heritage. Housed on the estate of the former Tuscan-style villa of the Duchess de Plaisance, the museum grounds are a little oasis in the urban chaos.

Christian art, dating from the 4th to 19th centuries and shedding light on Byzantine and post-Byzantine culture, is beautifully presented in themed displays in multilevel underground galleries. Artefacts from Greece and other reaches of the Byzantine empire include exquisite icons, early Christian sculptures, frescoes, mosaics, ceramics, wall paintings, Coptic embroideries, coins, jewellery and parchment manuscripts. Highlights include the Mytiline treasure, a precious collection of gold and silver ecclesiastical vestments and secular items, as well as Christian reliefs from the Parthenon and Christian temples on the Acropolis, and a 13th-century church-dome fresco.

At the time of writing the elegant mansion was being restored to house temporary exhibitions, a café and gift shop.

See also p111.

>ATHENS DIARY

Athens has a distinctly seasonal cultural life, with a busy year-round social calendar. Summer festivals are a highlight and from May to September there are concerts featuring top local performers and an impressive line-up of touring international acts. The historic centre takes on a festive atmosphere, with free concerts and events held in squares, amphitheatres, parks and public places, along with art exhibitions and book fairs. Winter is a time for live music in intimate venues and big clubs, theatre, opera and classical music. Events are often announced at the last minute, so check the local press or online at www.culture.gr, www.athensinfo guide.com or www.cityofathens.gr. For online bookings try Ticketnet (www.ticket net.gr), Ticketpro (www.ticketpro.gr) or Ticket Services (www.ticketservices.gr).

An impressive ceramic pot on exhibition at the distinguished National Archaeological Museum (p104), Exarhia

JANUARY

Epiphany

Young men dive to retrieve a cross thrown into the sea (winning a year's good luck) for the traditional blessing of the water (6 January) celebrations in Piraeus.

FEBRUARY

Apokries (Carnival)

Carnival festivities include 10 days of street parties, theatrical performances and traditional revelry, especially in Plaka. Look out for barbecue feasts on *Tsiknopempti* (Smokey Thursday).

ATHENS BIENNIAL

The inaugural **Athens Biennial** (www .athensbiennial.org) in 2007 added a major international contemporary art event to Athens' arts calendar. Look out for the next artistic dialogue scheduled to begin in June 2009, when local and international artists will put on art projects, exhibitions, performances and film screenings over the summer in various venues around Gazi (p88) and downtown.

MARCH

Independence Day

Greece's national day occurs on 25 March, when an impressive military parade makes

Theatre-goers preparing for a performance at the splendid Odeon of Herodes Atticus (p57)

its way to Plateia Syntagmatos (Syntagma Sq), celebrating Greek Independence.

APRIL

Easter

Usually held in March or April, evocative church services include Good Friday's candlelit procession and midnight Mass celebrations on Easter Saturday, which are particularly atmospheric in Plaka.

MAY

May Day

On 1 May Athenians head to the hills for spring picnics; Labour Day union rallies gather in the city centre (usually in Syntagma).

European Jazz Festival

www.cityofathens.gr

Bringing together jazz artists from more than 14 European countries, this festival has been expanding since it began in 2001. Free concerts are held over several nights at the Technopolis (p90), in Gazi, from 9pm to midnight.

Art Athina

www.art-athina.gr

Athens' annual three-day international contemporary art fair at the massive Hellexpo centre showcases a broad spectrum of art from Greek and international galleries, including sculpture and installations. Satellite exhibitions are also held in other venues.

JUNE

Athens Festival

www.greekfestival.gr

Greece's pre-eminent cultural festival summer program kicks off in venues around Athens; see below for more information.

Synch Festival

www.synch.gr

Innovative three-day international music and digital-arts festival at the Technopolis (p90) and other venues.

SUMMER FESTIVALS

The biggest cultural event is the **Athens Festival** (☎ 210 322 1459; www.hellenicfestival .gr), with performances held at the historic **Odeon of Herodes Atticus** (p57) and other venues around town. Tickets can be purchased from the Hellenic Festival box office (Map pp40–1, F3; Panepistimiou 39, Syntagma), which caters for the Athens Festival, the Epidavros theatre and music festivals and other events.

Eclectic summer music concerts are also held June to September at the outdoor amphitheatre on **Lykavittos Hill** (p111) and at stunning venues in former quarries during the **Vyronas Festival** (☎ 210 762 6438), and the **Petras Festival** (☎ 210 501 2402; Petroupoli) in western Athens.

JULY

Rockwave
www.rockwavefestival.gr
Rock fans gather at Terravibe, north of Athens, to see top international rock acts.

Athens International Dance Festival
www.cityofathens.gr
Contemporary dance performances by local and international ensembles, from Berlin to San Francisco, are held at the Technopolis (p90), along with parallel exhibitions and events.

AUGUST

Full Moon Festival
Every August full moon, the Acropolis (p52) stays open until late, and musical performances are held at the Roman Agora (p66) and other key archaeological sites.

SEPTEMBER

Athens International Film Festival
www.aiff.gr
An eclectic program of international and Greek independent cinema; for open-air cinemas see p160.

FASHION SHOW
Athens Fashion Week (www.hfda.gr) is actually two separate weeks of catwalk glamour as Greek designers showcase their spring (March) and autumn (October) collections in fashion extravaganzas at the Zappeio Palace (p44).

OCTOBER

Ohi Day
This national holiday is commemorated on 28 October, with parades to the Parliament that celebrate Metaxas' rejection of Mussolini's ultimatum to allow troops free passage through Greece in WWII.

NOVEMBER

Athens Marathon
www.athensclassicmarathon.gr
Runners follow the original 490 BC route from Marathon (east of Athens) run by the messenger heralding the defeat of the Persians, finishing at the Panathenaic Stadium (p125).

DECEMBER

Festive Season
www.christmasinathens.gr (in Greek)
Christmas festivities in Syntagma (p38), Plateia Kotzia (Kotzia Sq) in Omonia (p94) and other central squares. A New Year's Eve concert is held at Syntagma.

Playing with mirror magic at the Museum of Greek Children's Art (p64), Plaka

ITINERARIES

Most major sites and attractions in Athens are within close proximity, so you can pack plenty into a day, but it's worth venturing beyond the tourist sites to explore the city's many neighbourhoods. In summer, escape to cool museums in the middle of the day – or take a siesta to be in form for Athens' late-night dining culture and nightlife.

DAY ONE

Start with an early morning climb to the Acropolis (p52), winding your way down through the Ancient Agora (p62). Venture into the streets of Plaka, passing by the Roman Agora (p66) and the Turkish Baths (p67) before heading to the Monastiraki to initiate yourself with a souvlaki at Thanasis (p73). After exploring the Monastiraki Flea Market (p69), take in the atmosphere over a coffee at Dioskouri (p74). In the afternoon head to the new Acropolis Museum (p52) to see the treasures from the sacred rock, then take a long stroll along the pedestrian promenade, passing the Theatre of Dionysos (p53) and Odeon of Herodes Atticus (p57), climbing up to Filopappou Hill (Map pp78–9, D8) for the views, then winding around to the cafés and restaurants around Thisio (p82). Dine under the floodlit Acropolis, then head to the bars of Psyrri (p85) for a nightcap.

DAY TWO

Catch the changing of the guard ceremony (p43) at Parliament in Syntagma. Do some window-shopping in Kolonaki (p115) or people-watching at its trendy cafés, before heading to the Benaki Museum (p111), where you can lunch on the rooftop overlooking the National Gardens (p39). Stroll down to the old Panathenaic Stadium (p125) and then to the Temple of Olympian Zeus (p43) and Hadrian's Arch (p39). Dedicate the afternoon to seeing Greece's most significant antiquities at the National Archaeological Museum (p104), heading to bohemian Exarhia (p102) for an afternoon drink. Take the funicular railway up Lykavittos Hill (p111) at sunset for impressive panoramic views of Athens. Head to Gazi (p88) for dinner at one of the trendy tavernas and a drink at one of the popular bars.

Top left Romancing the night away along the Ancient Promenade (p13) **Top right** Admiring the ancient ruins lying beneath the new Acropolis Museum (p52) **Bottom** Preparing delicious souvlaki at Thanasis (p73)

DAY THREE

Get another dose of culture at the Goulandris Museum of Cycladic & Ancient Greek Art (p114), the Byzantine & Christian Museum (p111) or the National Art Gallery (p124). Take in lunch at one of the tavernas around the Athens Central Market (p96) and then go shopping in Ermou (Map pp78–9, E3) or Plaka (p67). Take the scenic tram along the coast (p142), walk along the seafront promenade, stopping at one of the cafés or restaurants along the waterfront, perhaps taking a refreshing dip in the sea. Any time of year, head to Piraeus for seafood on the picturesque harbour of Mikrolimano (p134), followed by a drink at one of the nearby bars (p136). For summer nightlife head to one of the big beach clubs (p160), or in winter catch some live music at a *rembetika* (Greek blues) club (p161).

ATHENS FOR FREE

Walk around the archaeological park that is Athens, particularly around the promenade up to the Hill of the Pnyx (Map pp78–9, C6) and Filopap-pou Hill (Map pp78–9, D8) and through Plaka (p58). Interesting free museums include the Museum of Greek Popular Instruments (p65), the Melina Mercouri Cultural Centre (p80), the War Museum (p114) and the Epigraphical Museum (p104). Major archaeological sites (including the Acropolis) and state museums are free on national holidays and Sundays between November and March, and the first Sunday of every month (except July, August and September). Free events are held at the

---

FORWARD PLANNING

Three weeks before you go Greeks are the masters of last-minute organisation and are not into planning their social lives too far ahead, but if you want to go to any big-ticket events check online. Tickets for the Athens Festival (p27) performances go on sale online three weeks before the event – booking for the Odeon of Herodes Atticus (Herodion; p57) is highly recommended. Other than that, it's the sort of city where you can get there and go with the flow.

One week before you go You won't be the only one wanting to dine with Acropolis views, so secure a prime table at rooftop terrace restaurants, such as Kuzina (p83) and Filistron (p82), or fine-dining establishments such as Varoulko (p84) and Pil Poul (p83), especially if you're here over a weekend or in the peak of summer. Check out opening times of smaller museums, as many close early, and be wary of local store hours if you plan to shop (eg never on a Sunday) anywhere other than in the tourist strips.

Technopolis (p90) and around Thisio metro (Map pp78–9, D3). Syntagma metro is like a mini-museum (see Underground Art, p42), while the Athens Central Market (p96) and Monastiraki Flea Market (p69) are fun to explore.

ESCAPE THE HEAT

Explore the archaeological sites early, taking refuge from the heat as you explore the National Archaeological Museum (p14) and other museums in the middle of the day. Alternatively head to the sites in the late afternoon, as the Acropolis and other key attractions are open until 7pm in summer. Get an air-conditioned virtual tour through ancient Greece at the Hellenic Cosmos (p91) before taking the air-conditioned tram to a nearby beach (p142) for a refreshing swim and break at a beach bar. After a late-afternoon siesta, take the funicular up to Lykavittos Hill (p111) for cool breezes and panoramic views. After dark, dine on a rooftop terrace, such as Kuzina (p83). See a late session in the gardens at the Aigli (p48) open-air cinema or head to the Akrotiri Boutique (p146) or Balux (p145) clubs along the beach.

A quaint alley and the whitewashed stone architecture of the Anafiotika quarter (p16)

NEIGHBOURHOODS

'The way to enjoy Athens is not to visit here for five days, but to live here for five days,' author Patricia Storace so eloquently opined. Athens is best appreciated by delving beneath the surface and getting to know its diverse neighbourhoods.

Athens at first sight can no doubt be a shock to the senses, a confronting, seemingly monotonous concrete mass of sprawling apartment blocks. But once you enter the historic centre, the city becomes far less intimidating. At heart, Athens is a city of distinctive village-like neighbourhoods.

Central Athens is best explored on foot. The historic centre, main archaeological sites, major landmarks, museums and attractions are within a short distance of each other. Compact neighbourhoods mesh into each other, yet within a few short blocks offer an entirely different experience – from the chic boutiques and cafés of ever-fashionable Kolonaki you can walk to the graffiti-splashed streets of bohemian Exarhia.

Downtown Athens is a virtual triangle incorporating Syntagma, the city's central hub, the commercial district around Omonia and the market quarter leading to the colourful flea market at Monastiraki.

The picturesque streets of Plaka, under the Acropolis, are the first port of call for most tourists, who drift to the bars of nearby Psyrri in the evening. The city's nightlife scene has moved on to gay-friendly Gazi, where a new cultural precinct is developing along Pireos. Keramikos and Metaxourghio are the emerging new hotspots, with galleries and restaurants slowly moving into the area as part of the centre's revitalisation and gradual gentrification.

The sprawling suburbs need more time for exploration. Leafy Kifisia is where the old money is; the harbours of Piraeus offer a unique ambience at night; while Glyfada and the coast are popular summer destinations.

AMBELOKIPI

ILISSIA

EXARHIA

Exarhia (p103)

OMONIA

Omonia & Metaxourghio (p95)

Kolonaki (pp112–13)

KOLONAKI

SYNTAGMA

Syntagma (pp40–1)

MONASTIRAKI

PLAKA

PANGRATI

Mets & Pangrati (p123)

METS

To Glyfada & the Coast (p143) (15km)

PSYRRI

Plaka & Monastiraki (pp60–1)

ANAFIOTIKA

MAKRYGIANNI

Akropoli & Makrygianni (p51)

KERAMIKOS

THISIO

Psyrri, Thisio & Keramikos (pp78–9)

KOUKAKI

GAZI

Gazi & Rouf (p89)

ROUF

To Piraeus (pp132–3) (9km)

(18km)

0   1 km

0   0.5 miles

>SYNTAGMA

Syntagma is the heart of modern Athens, with Plateia Syntagmatos (Constitution Sq) its historic meeting point and transport hub. The grand square, with its fountains and cafés, overlooks the majestic Parliament, where crowds gather to watch the changing of the guard ceremony. It's surrounded by the central business district, main shopping areas, top hotels, museums and embassies.

Syntagma is the focal point for Athens' political and civic life, from protest rallies to New Year's celebrations. The square is a good place to get your bearings, with the landmark Hotel Grand Bretagne on one side and the Ermou shopping strip opposite Parliament.

You can reach most major attractions on foot or catch the metro from Syntagma's showpiece underground station. The National Gardens offer a welcome respite from the hustle and bustle, or it's a short walk to the quieter streets of Plaka. Hip new bars, on Kolokotroni and tucked in tiny alleys, are part of the resurgence of downtown Athens.

SYNTAGMA

◉ SEE

Athens Academy	1	B2
Athens University	2	A2
City of Athens Museum	3	B4
Hadrian's Arch	4	G6
Megaron Maximou	5	G1
National Gardens	6	G3
National Historical Museum	7	C3
National Library	8	A2
Numismatic Museum	9	C2
Parliament	10	E2
Presidential Palace	11	H1
Roman Baths	12	G5
Temple of Olympian Zeus	13	H6
Tomb of the Unknown Soldier	14	E3
Zappeio Gardens & Palace	15	H4

🛍 SHOP

Aidini	16	E5
Apriati	17	D5
Aristokratikon	18	D4
Attica	19	C2
Cellier	20	D2
Ekavi	21	D5
Eleftheroudakis	22	C2
Folli-Follie	23	C5
Lalaounis	24	D2
Mastiha Shop	25	D2
Spiliopoulos	26	B6
Zolotas	27	C3
Zoumboulakis Gallery	28	D2

🍴 EAT

Ariston	29	C4
Cibus	30	H3
Furin Kazan	31	E4
Kostas	32	B6
Lena's Bio	33	E4
Miniatura	34	B5
Tzitzikas & Mermingas	35	D4

🍸 DRINK

7 Jokers	36	C4
Bartessera	37	B4
Booze Cooperativa	38	B5
Galaxy	39	C3

★ PLAY

Aigli	40	H4
Apollon & Attikon	41	B3
Lallabai	42	H4

Please see over for map

SEE

CITY OF ATHENS MUSEUM

☎ 210 324 6164; www.athenscitymu
seum.gr; Paparigopoulou 5 & 7; admission €3; ⏱ 9am-4pm Mon & Wed-Fri,
10-3pm Sat & Sun; Ⓜ Panepistimio

Once the residence of King Otto
and Queen Amalia, the museum
displays some of the royal couple's
personal effects and furniture –
including the throne – as well as
paintings by leading Greek and
foreign artists and models of 19th-
century Athens.

NATIONAL GARDENS

☎ 210 721 5019; Leoforos Vasilissis Amalias; ⏱ 7am-dusk; Ⓜ Syntagma; ♿

MARKING YOUR TURF

Roman emperor Hadrian erected **Hadrian's Arch** (cnr Leoforos Vasilissis Olgas
& Leoforos Vasilissis Amalias) in AD 132,
probably to commemorate the conse-
cration of the Temple of Olympian Zeus.
But the arch was also a dividing point
between the ancient and Roman city.
The northwest frieze bears the inscrip-
tion 'This is Athens, the Ancient city of
Theseus', while the other side of the
frieze states 'This is the city of Hadrian,
and not of Theseus'.

The former royal gardens,
designed by Queen Amalia, are
a great green refuge during the
summer. Winding paths lead to

Taking refuge from the heat under a shady alcove at the National Gardens

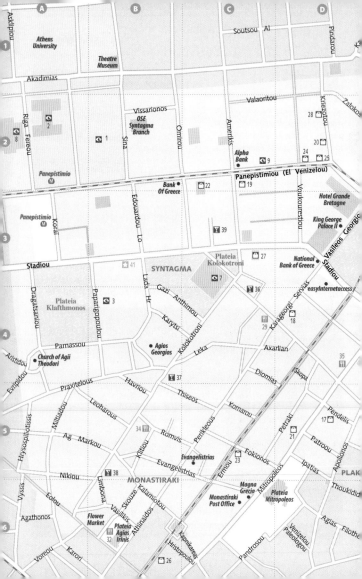

NEIGHBOURHOODS SYNTAGMA

Pedestal of the Temple of Olympian Zeus (opposite)

ornamental ponds with waterfowl and there's a pleasant café near Irodou Attikou.

NATIONAL HISTORICAL MUSEUM

☎ 210 323 7617; Stadiou 13, Plateia Kolokotroni; admission €3, free Sun; 9am-2pm Tue-Sun; M Syntagma
Greece's first parliament building houses memorabilia from the War of Independence, including Byron's helmet and sword, weapons, costumes and flags, paintings, Byzantine and medieval exhibits, and photos illustrating Greece's evolution since Constantinople's fall in 1453.

NUMISMATIC MUSEUM

☎ 210 364 3774; Panepistimiou 12; admission €3; 8.30am-3pm Tue-Sun; M Syntagma;
Even if you have scant interest in its fine coin collection, this exemplary neoclassical building has some beautiful frescoes and mosaic floors and a shady café in the garden. It was once the home of renowned archaeologist Heinrich Schliemann, who excavated Troy and Mycenae.

PRESIDENTIAL PALACE & MEGARON MAXIMOU

Irodou Attikou; M Syntagma
Evzones (guards) stand guard outside Ernst Ziller's imposing 1870s former royal palace, now the residence of Greece's president. Neighbouring Megaron Maximou, an elegant neoclassical building easily spotted by the media throng outside, is the prime

UNDERGROUND ART

Athens' splendid metro stations are underground museums and galleries, exhibiting art installations by leading Greek artists and archaeological finds uncovered during the metro's construction. Look out for Alekos Fassianos' work at Metaxourghio, Yiannis Gaïtis' trademark men at Larisis and New York—based artist Stephen Antonakos' neon installation at Evangelismos.

CHANGING OF THE GUARD

Every hour, on the hour, towering *evzones* (guards) in traditional uniforms of short kilts and pom-poms march up to Greece's **Parliament** (Plateia Syntagmatos; Ⓜ Syntagma) for the colourful, high-kicking changing of the guard ceremony. The rest of the time, they amuse the crowds by standing stock-still 24/7 whilst guarding the **Tomb of the Unknown Soldier**. On Sundays and major holidays, there's a fancier affair (10.45am) in full regalia with a military band.

minister's residence. Admission is by invitation only.

Ⓞ TEMPLE OF OLYMPIAN ZEUS

☎ 210 922 6330; Leoforos Vasilissis Olgas; admission €2 (free with Acropolis pass); ⏰ 8am-7pm Apr-Oct, 8am-5pm Nov-Mar; Ⓜ Akropoli

The colossal Temple of Olympian Zeus (or Olympeion) is the largest in Greece and took more than 700 years to build. Fifteen of the original 104 massive (17m-high) Corinthian columns survive, along with the one that toppled over in a gale in 1852. Peisistratos began

Evzones (guards) marching at the Tomb of the Unknown Soldier after the changing of the guard ceremony

> ## NEOCLASSICAL ATHENS
>
> After Greek independence, the new capital was rebuilt in the spirit of ancient Greece, boasting the finest neoclassical architecture in Europe. The 1885 **Athens Academy** (Panepistimiou), flanked by Apollo and Athena standing on two giant columns, is part of the architectural legacy of the Danish brothers Theophile and Christian Hansen. Theophile designed the adjacent 1902 **National Library** (☎ 210 338 2541; Riga Fereou; 🕑 9am-8pm Mon-Thu, 9am-2pm Fri & Sat), which has a stunning reading room, while the **Athens University** (Riga Fereou) is Christian's work. Hansen student Ernst Ziller followed through with the grand National Theatre of Greece (p100), the Stathatos Mansion (which forms part of the Museum of Cycladic & Ancient Greek Art, p114) and Numismatic Museum (p42).
>
> Unfortunately, many of Athens' neoclassical buildings fell victim to the city's rapid expansions, knocked down to make way for bland apartment blocks or left crumbling by inheritance disputes.

building the temple in the 6th century BC on the western bank of the Ilissos River, at the site of a smaller temple (590–560 BC) dedicated to the cult of Olympian Zeus (its foundations can be seen on the site), but construction stalled due to lack of funds. A succession of leaders tried to finish the job, making adjustments along the way, which explains inconsistencies in the temple. Hadrian finally finished the task in AD 131. The temple housed a giant gold and ivory statue of Zeus and one of Hadrian.

🟢 ZAPPEIO GARDENS & PALACE

Leoforos Vasilissis Amalias; Ⓜ **Syntagma;** ♿ 🚻

Men still gather to play backgammon in the leafy gardens surrounding the majestic Zappeio palace, built in the 1870s by the wealthy Greek-Romanian benefactor Konstantinos Zappas. The palace courtyard is stunning and there's a peaceful café and the historic Aigli cinema (p48) nearby.

🛍 SHOP

🔲 AIDINI *Artisan*

☎ **210 323 4591; Nikis 32;** Ⓜ **Syntagma**
Artisan Errikos Aidini's unique metal creations are made in his workshop at the back of this charming store, including small mirrors, candlesticks, lamps, planes and his signature bronze boats.

🔲 APRIATI *Jewellery & Ceramics*

☎ **210 322 9020; www.apriati.com; Pendelis 9 (cnr Mitropoleos);** Ⓜ **Syntagma**
This tiny, delightful store has a tempting selection of fun and original contemporary designs from Athena Axioti, Themis Bobolas and

other local designers. There's a second store in Kolonaki (p115).

☐ ARISTOKRATIKON *Chocolate*
☎ 210 322 0546; Karageorgi Servias 9; Ⓜ Syntagma

Chocaholics will be thrilled by the dazzling array of handmade chocolates at this tiny store. Not one for the weak-willed. Also try the pistachio clusters.

☐ ATTICA *Department Store*
☎ 211 180 2500; Panepistimiou 7; ⏲ 10am-9pm Mon-Fri, 10am-7pm Sat; Ⓜ Syntagma

This upmarket department store in the Citylink complex (which houses top fashion labels and jewellers) has eight levels crammed with leading brands, hip clothing, cosmetics and designer temptations.

☐ CELLIER *Wine*
☎ 210 361 0040; Kriezotou 1; Ⓜ Syntagma

A delectable collection of some of Greece's best wines and liqueurs, with knowledgeable staff to explain Greek varieties and winemakers, and boxed gift packs.

☐ EKAVI *Boardgames*
☎ 210 323 7740; www.manopoulos .com; Mitropoleos 36; Ⓜ Syntagma

If you're hooked on the local sport, there's a huge selection of

backgammon boards, as well as great chess pieces depicting the battles of Troy, the Ottomans vs the Byzantines and other themes.

☐ ELEFTHEROUDAKIS *Books & Music*
☎ 210 331 4180; Panepistimiou 17; ⏲ 9am-9pm Mon-Fri, 9am-6pm Sat; Ⓜ Panepistimio

A seven-storey bibliophile's paradise with the widest selection of books from and about Greece, plus English-language books, including maps and travel guides, and a top-floor café. There's a branch in Plaka (p68).

☐ FOLLI-FOLLIE *Jewellery & Accessories*
☎ 210 323 0601; www.folli-follie.com; Ermou 37; Ⓜ Syntagma

This successful global Greek chain has a wide range of fashionable watches, bijoux jewellery, shawls, leather bags and accessories. There are stores around town.

☐ LALAOUNIS *Jewellery*
☎ 210 361 1371; Panepistimiou 6 (cnr Voukourestiou); Ⓜ Syntagma

Leading Greek jeweller Lalaounis' exquisitely crafted creations reflect ancient Greek motifs and draw inspiration from other cultures, biology, nature and mythology. Lalaounis also has a jewellery museum (p53).

🏠 MASTIHA SHOP
Speciality Products

☎ 210 363 2750; www.mastihashop.
com; Panepistimiou 6; ⏰ 9am-9pm;
Ⓜ Syntagma

Mastic, the medicinal resin from
rare mastic trees produced only
on the island of Chios, is the key
ingredient in everything in this
store, including smartly packaged
natural skin products, essential
oils, food products, pharmaceu-
ticals and a liqueur that's divine
when served chilled.

🏠 SPILIOPOULOS *Shoes & Bags*
☎ 210 322 7590; Ermou 63; Ⓜ Syntagma

Chaos reigns but you may find a
bargain among the overcrowded
racks of imported designer sec-
onds and old-season shoes and
bags. It also stocks leather jackets.
There's a branch in Monastiraki
(p70).

🏠 ZOLOTAS *Jewellery*
☎ 210 331 3320; Stadiou 9; Ⓜ Syntagma

Internationally renowned Zolotas
breathes life into ancient Greece
with replicas of museum pieces,
having had the exclusive rights
to make copies of the real thing
since 1972.

🏠 ZOUMBOULAKIS GALLERY
Art

☎ 210 363 4454; Kriezotou 7;
Ⓜ Syntagma

An excellent range of limited-
edition prints and posters by
leading Greek artists, including
Tsarouhis, Mytara and Fassianos.

🍴 EAT

🍴 ARISTON *Pies*   €
☎ 210 322 7626; Voulis 10;
Ⓜ Syntagma

Since 1910 this place has been
baking the best fresh *tyropites*
(cheese pies), the perfect snack on
the run. Try its renowned *kourou*
(thick type of pastry) variety or
one of the many other tasty fill-
ings, such as red peppers, mush-
rooms, chicken or spinach.

🍴 CIBUS
Italian, Mediterranean   €€€

☎ 210 336 9364; Zappeio Gardens;
⏰ lunch & dinner; Ⓜ Syntagma

Located in the cool Zappeio Gardens (in the Aigli cinema complex
next to the palace), Cibus does
superb contemporary Italian-style
cuisine in an elegant modern
setting.

🍴 FURIN KAZAN
Japanese   €€

☎ 210 322 9170; Apollonos 2; ⏰ lunch
& dinner Mon-Sat; Ⓜ Syntagma

Japanese tourists regularly fill
this café-style restaurant before a
second shift of adventurous Greek
diners descend for decent sushi
and authentic Japanese food.

🍴 KOSTAS *Souvlaki* €
☎ 210 323 2971; Plateia Agia Irinis 2; ⏱ 5am-5pm; Ⓜ Monastiraki
On a pleasant square opposite Agia Irini church, this old-style virtual hole-in-the wall joint churns out tasty souvlaki and kebabs, with its signature spicy tomato sauce.

🍴 LENA'S BIO *Café-deli* €
☎ 210 324 1360; Nikis 11; ⏱ 8am-6pm Mon-Fri; ⏱ 8am-4pm Sat; Ⓜ Syntagma
There are only a few seats inside, but this is a great place for wholesome organic food, snacks and salads, as well as a range of fresh produce and deli items to take away.

🍴 MINIATURA *Taverna* €
☎ 210 323 3459; Romvis 21; ⏱ Mon-Sat; Ⓜ Syntagma
A quaint family-run little taverna tucked away in a side street, this is a great place for traditional homestyle fare, with regularly changing daily specials at very reasonable prices.

🍴 TZITZIKAS & MERMINGAS *Mezedhopoleio* €€
☎ 210 324 7607; Mitropoleos 12-14; ⏱ lunch & dinner; Ⓜ Syntagma
This bright and cheery modern mezedhopoleio is popular for its delicious and creative mezedhes. The old Greek deli theme extends from the walls of shelves lined with Greek products to the unique toilet hand basins.

🍸 DRINK

🍸 7 JOKERS *Café-bar*
☎ 210 321 9225; Voulis 7; ⏱ 10am-late; Ⓜ Syntagma
This small, friendly bar right in central Athens is a good place for a coffee by day or a quiet early drink, but the vibe steps up several notches way into the night.

🍸 BARTESSERA *Café-bar*
☎ 210 322 9805; Kolokotroni 25; ⏱ 11am-late; Ⓜ Syntagma
Tucked at the end of a narrow arcade off Kolokotroni, with a quirky central courtyard, this friendly place is a little oasis by day and a lively bar at night, with a hip 30-something crowd, guest DJs and art exhibitions.

🍸 BOOZE COOPERATIVA *Café-bar*
☎ Kolokotroni 57; ⏱ 10am-late Mon-Fri, from 3pm Sat, from noon Sun; Ⓜ Monastiraki
By day, this laid-back arty hangout is full of hip young Athenians playing chess and backgammon and working on their Macs (with free wi-fi) on the 6m-long table; later it transforms into a happening bar that rocks till late. The basement

ROMAN BATHS

Excavations for a metro ventilation shaft revealed the well-preserved ruins of a large Roman bath complex near Syntagma. Now on display under protective cover, the Roman Baths, which extend into the National Gardens, were established near the Ilissos River after the Herulian raids in the 3rd century AD; the baths were destroyed and repaired again in the 5th or 6th century.

hosts art exhibitions and there's a theatre upstairs.

⛒ GALAXY *Bar*

☎ 210 322 7733; Stadiou 10; ⏱ 10am-late; Ⓜ Syntagma

Not to be mistaken for the Hilton's impressive rooftop Galaxy bar, this tiny place in an obscure arcade is a friendly, time-warp type of place where you sit at the bar and get great service and a little meze with each round.

⭐ PLAY

⭐ AIGLI *Cinema*

☎ 210 336 9369; Zappeio Gardens; tickets €8; Ⓜ Syntagma

One of Athens' oldest and most delightful outdoor cinemas is in the middle of the gardens, ideal for a balmy night enjoying a flick with a glass of wine.

⭐ APOLLON & ATTIKON *Cinema*

☎ 210 323 6811; Stadiou 19; tickets €9; Ⓜ Panepistimio

The beautifully restored Apollon, a historic 1960s theatre, and the At-

The entrance to the charming outdoor cinema, Aigli

tikon just next door, operate year-round showing the latest releases. The cinemas also host the Athens International Film Festival (p28).

LALLABAI *Bar-restaurant*
☎ 210 336 9340; Zappeio Gardens; admission €10 Sun-Thu, €15 Fri & Sat; ⏱ 9pm-late; Ⓜ Syntagma

A stylish and cool (literally) bar-restaurant set among the trees in the middle of the Zappeio Gardens, with comfy loungers and ever-changing décor. There's mainstream music and a slick, glam crowd, as well as a small but eclectic menu.

>AKROPOLI & MAKRYGIANNI

The area around the southern slope of the Acropolis has had a new lease of life since the creation of the grand pedestrian promenade and the Akropoli metro station. Lined with graceful buildings, the promenade is bustling with tourists heading to the Acropolis, families strolling, kids riding their bikes, and dressed-up patrons heading to a show at the Odeon of Herodes Atticus. The newest star attraction is the Acropolis Museum, a massive modernist edifice next to the old military hospital now housing the Acropolis study centre and culture ministry offices.

Despite their proximity to the historic centre, the quiet neighbourhoods south of the Acropolis are refreshingly untouristy. Though Makrygianni has several hotels, restaurants and small museums, the area is mostly residential, with some lovely restored neoclassical mansions in the coveted streets below the Acropolis. Koukaki, which runs along the foothills of Filopappou Hill, has some excellent neighbourhood tavernas, as does nearby Ano Petralona (p85).

AKROPOLI & MAKRYGIANNI

◎ SEE
Acropolis 1 B2
Acropolis Museum 2 C4
Atelier Spyros Vasiliou ...3 A4
Ilias Lalaounis Jewellery
 Museum 4 B4
Parthenon 5 B2
Theatre of
 Dionysos.....................6 C3

🛍 SHOP
Greece Is For Lovers........7 B4
Kanakis...........................8 C4

🍴 EAT
Aglio, Olio &
 Peperoncino................9 D4
Mani Mani 10 C5
Strofi............................11 A4

▼ DRINK
Duente..........................12 D3
Tike Athens..................13 C5

★ PLAY
Lamda Club 14 D4
Odeon of Herodes
 Atticus.......................15 A3
Small Music Theatre.....16 B5

ANAFIOTIKA

Acropolis

Ancient Agora

Mitroou
Panos
Tholou
Thrasyvoulou
Lyssiou
Erotokritou
Fiessa
Sholiou
Tripodon
Kekropos
Klepsydras
Aretousas
Kanellopoulos Museum
Prytaniou
Theorias
Hill

Kydathineon
Plateia Filomousou Eterias
Erechtheion
Rangava
Afroditis
Adrianou
Herefontos
Stratonos
Galanou
Acropolis ⓘ 1
Parthenon ⓘ 5
Old Acropolis Museum
Thespidos
Mado
Epimenidou
Lysikratous
Frynihou
Eshinou
Thrasyllou
Vakhou
Vyronos
Odeon of Herodes Atticus ★ 15
ⓘ 6
Theatre of Dionysos
To Dora Stratou Dance Theatre 1.5km
Theorias
Stoa of Eumenes
Entrance to Theatre of Dionysos/Acropolis

ilopappou Hill
Dionysiou Areopagitou
Webster
Rovertou Galli
Kallisperi
Akropoli Ⓜ
Tzireon
ⓘ 12
4 ⓘ
Propyleon
Acropolis View
Fratti
Angelikara
Ratzieri
Thiramenous
Fenaretiou
Sofroniskou
ⓘ 3 ⓘ 11
Karyatidon
Mitseon
MAKRYGIANNI
Akropoli Ⓜ
Diakou
Stratigou Makrygianni
Potmou
Ath
To Hop In Sightseeing (50m)
Kaleshrou
Promahou
Kavalloti
Erehthiou
Parthenos
ⓘ 7
ⓘ 2
Lembesi
ⓘ 9
Plateia Tsokri
ⓘ 14
Hatzihristou
Mitromara
Zitrou
Strateon
Petmeza
Vouravhi
Koryzi
Nezer Hr
Tosif Rogon
Tsami Karatasi
Hera Hotel
ⓘ 13
Drakou
Liakou
Falirou
ⓘ 10
Veikou
Church of Agios Ioannis
Donda Sp
Negri Th
noghanni
Zaharitsa
Gioni
ⓘ 16
Stratigou Kondouli
Falirou
Leof Syngrou Andrea
Leof Syngrou Andrea
Kallirrois
Botsari Noti
Botsari Markou
Plateia Gargarettas
Tourist Police
Dimitrakopoulou N
Androutsou Od
Dilados
Kallirrois
Theofilopoulou
Plateia Agios Pandeleimonos
To Post Office (50m)
To Edodi (250m)
Ⓜ Syngrou-Fix
Alkimou
Inglesi
Tymfristou
Sismani
Iras
Menexhou
Plateia Kynosargous

⊙ SEE

⊙ ACROPOLIS

☎ 210 321 0219; www.culture.gr; Akropoli; admission €12 (valid 4 days & includes entrance to Roman & Ancient Agoras, Keramikos, Temple of Olympian Zeus & Theatre of Dionysos); 🕑 8am-7pm Apr-Oct, 8am-5pm Nov-Mar; Ⓜ Akropoli; ♿

The magnificent Acropolis defines and dominates Athens. Unlike other cities where the main attractions are on the outskirts of town, the sacred rock on which the ancient Greek temples were built rises spectacularly above the centre of the city. The main entrance is from Dionysiou Areopagitou near the Odeon of Herodes Atticus, or from Theorias if you're coming from Plaka (there's another entrance near the Kanellopoulos Museum). Large bags must be left at the main entrance cloakroom. See p10 for more details.

⊙ ACROPOLIS MUSEUM

☎ 210 924 1043; www.newacropolis museum.gr; Akropoli; Ⓜ Akropoli; ♿

The showpiece museum houses the original marbles and sculptures from the Acropolis (see p12 for details). The museum was in the process of completion at the time of writing. See also the interview with the museum's curator (p54).

The magnificent Theatre of Dionysos (p53) hosted dramas written by Aeschylus, Sophocles and Euripides

ATELIER SPYROS VASSILIOU

☎ 210 923 1502; www.spyrosvassiliou.org; Webster 5a, Akropoli; admission €4; ⏰ 10am-8pm Mon-Fri, 10am-3pm Sat & Sun (closed mid-Aug); Ⓜ Thisio or Akropoli

The home and studio of leading 20th-century Greek painter and set designer Spyros Vassiliou (1902–1985) has been converted into an impressive museum and archive of his work. Exhibits include his celebrated paintings depicting urban Athens, theatre sets, his artist's tools and illustrations from literary journals and newspapers.

ILIAS LALAOUNIS JEWELLERY MUSEUM

☎ 210 922 1044; www.lalaounis-jewelry museum.gr; Kallisperi 12 (cnr Karyatidon), Makrygianni; admission €4 (free 3-9pm Wed & 9-11am Sat); ⏰ 9am-4pm Mon & Thu-Sat, 9am-9pm Wed, 11am-4pm Sun; Ⓜ Akropoli

Jewellery and decorative arts inspired by various periods in Greek history showcase the talents of Greece's renowned jeweller Ilias Lalaounis. The museum demonstrates jewellery-making techniques from prehistoric times. The permanent collection includes thematic displays of more than 4000 pieces of jewellery and intricate microsculptures designed by Lalaounis since the 1940s. The museum also hosts temporary exhibitions and runs cultural programs dedicated to the art.

THEATRE OF DIONYSOS

☎ 210 322 4625; Dionysiou Areopagitou, Akropoli; admission €2 (free with Acropolis pass); ⏰ 8am-7pm Apr-Oct, 8am-5pm Nov-Mar; Ⓜ Akropoli

The original 6th-century timber theatre was built on the site of the Festival of the Great Dionysia. During Athens' golden age, the theatre hosted productions of the works of Aeschylus, Sophocles, Euripides and Aristophanes. Reconstructed in stone and marble between 342 and 326 BC, the theatre had seating for more than 17,000 spectators (spread over 64 tiers, of which only about 20 tiers survive) and an altar to Dionysos in the orchestra pit. The Pentelic marble thrones on the lower levels were for dignitaries and priests – including a grand one in the centre for the Priest of Dionysos, identifiable by the lions' paws, satyrs and griffins carved on the back.

🛍 SHOP

GREECE IS FOR LOVERS
Designer Souvenirs

☎ 210 924 5064; www.greeceisforlovers.com; 13a Karyatidon, Akropoli; ⏰ 10am-6pm Mon-Fri, 11am-3pm Sat; Ⓜ Akropoli

This is a tiny showroom where young designers play on the kitsch, from Corinthian column

Alexandros Mantis
Curator, new Acropolis Museum (p52)

Why the museum is important We've been waiting for 40 years to have a museum specifically designed to house the masterpieces from the Acropolis. **Best design feature** The exhibition space is 10 times bigger than the old museum. Visitors see the sculptures up close from all angles and the natural light really brings them to life. The Caryatids are no longer behind glass because we have the technology to protect them. **What visitors will see** We've transferred 355 pieces from the sacred rock and 4500 from storage. **Museum highlights** The 3rd-floor Parthenon Gallery, where you can see the marbles as they once were and gaze at the Acropolis at the same time. You can see all the missing pieces and which foreign museum has them. **Will the marbles ever return from London?** The new museum will be a dynamic force that will speak for itself.

dumb-bells, crocheted iPod covers and Aphrodite bust candles. Look for the giant Grecian sandal skateboard in the window.

 KANAKIS *Jewellery*
☎ 210 922 8297; Stratigou Makrygianni 17, Makrygianni; Ⓜ Akropoli
A stunning range of contemporary jewellery from Cretan Spiros Kanakis, who often plays on ancient Greek motifs in his original gold designs; mostly handmade in his Iraklio workshop.

🍴 EAT

🍴 **AGLIO, OLIO & PEPERONCINO** *Italian*   €€
☎ 210 921 1801; Porinou 13, Makrygianni; Ⓨ noon-midnight Mon-Fri, 8pm-2am Sat, 2-7pm Sun; Ⓜ Akropoli

Hardly the most obvious or inviting place for a restaurant, but this hidden gem behind the metro is a great choice for no-frills classic Italian cuisine. It's a great place for good-value pastas with authentic Italian flavours and a cosy, trattoria ambience.

🍴 **EDODI**
Modern Greek, International   €€€
off map, A6; ☎ 210 921 3013; Veikou 80, Koukaki; Ⓨ dinner Mon-Sat, closed Aug; Ⓜ Syngrou-Fix
For a special night out, book a table at tiny Edodi, where waiters parade a tantalising 'live' menu of the day's creative (but yet-to-be cooked) dishes. Impeccable service and delicious food in an elegant neoclassical building.

Kitchy merchandise with a message, for sale in Greece is For Lovers (p53)

MANI MANI
Modern Greek €€

☎ 210 921 8180; Falirou 10, Makrygianni; ⏰ 8pm-1am Tue-Sat, 2-5pm Sun; Ⓜ Akropoli

In a welcoming setting on the 1st floor of this charming neoclassical building, you'll enjoy excellent contemporary Greek cuisine. The menu includes dishes inspired by regional specialities from Mani, in the southern Peloponnese, such as the *loukaniko* (sausage) with orange, *siglino* (cured pork) or stewed pork with celery.

STROFI *Taverna* €€

☎ 210 921 4130; Rovertou Galli 25, Akropoli; ⏰ dinner Mon-Sat; Ⓜ Akropoli

This charming old-style taverna's rooftop terrace has superb Acropolis views, and a reasonable array of taverna classics. It used to be a hang-out for theatre performers, as the photos of its famous guests attest.

DRINK
DUENTE *Bar*

☎ 210 924 7069; Tzireon 2, Akropoli; ⏰ 6pm-late; Ⓜ Akropoli

An established local haunt, this intimate French brasserie–style bar with sedate music and a mature crowd is ideal for a quiet meal or drink at the bar.

TIKI ATHENS *Bar-restaurant*

☎ 210 923 6908; Falirou 15, Makrygianni; ⏰ 9pm-late; Ⓜ Akropoli

Funky '50s décor, an Asian-inspired menu, and an alternative hip, young crowd make this a fun place for a drink. Sample the impressive cocktail list to eclectic sounds ranging from jazz and rockabilly to Tom Waits.

PLAY
DORA STRATOU DANCE THEATRE *Dance*

off map, A3; ☎ administrative office 210 324 4395, theatre 210 921 4650; www .grdance.org; Filopappou Hill; tickets €15 ⏰ performances 9.30pm Tue-Sat & 8.15pm Sun May-Sep; ⓢ 15

Each summer since 1965, lively Greek folk-dance performances have been held at the open-air theatre on Filopappou Hill by this leading dance troupe. Some of the elaborate costumes are museum pieces.

LAMDA CLUB *Nightclub*

☎ 210 942 4202; Lembesi 15 (cnr Syngrou), Makrygianni; ⏰ closed Aug; Ⓜ Akropoli

Despite the gay scene drifting to Gazi, this three-level gay club is still one of the busiest in Athens, attracting a diverse late-night crowd. Pop, house and Greek music dominate, with two basement-dark rooms.

☆ ODEON OF HERODES ATTICUS *Theatre*

☎ 210 324 1807; www.hellenicfestival.gr; Dionysiou Areopagitou, Akropoli; Ⓜ Akropoli

This historic Roman amphitheatre, known as the Herodion (p21), is the preeminent arts venue in Athens and hosts the major events of the Athens Festival (p27).

☆ SMALL MUSIC THEATRE *Live Music*

☎ 210 924 5644; www.smallmusictheatre.gr; Veïkou 33, Koukaki; ⊙ from 9pm, performances from 10pm; Ⓜ Syngrou-Fix

This intimate venue hosts an interesting assortment of avant-garde bands and experimental music, including rock, jazz and electronic music.

>PLAKA & MONASTIRAKI

The oldest and most atmospheric neighbourhoods of Athens extend from busy Monastiraki to the picturesque streets of Plaka, on the eastern edge of the Acropolis. Plaka has an undeniable charm. Its paved, narrow streets pass by ancient sites, restored and crumbling neoclassical mansions, fascinating small museums, Byzantine churches and ambient tavernas. See also p16.

The main streets, Kydathineon and Adrianou, are lined with kitsch souvenir stores, but wandering off the tourist strip, you get a glimpse of old Athens – virtually car-free streets and the island-style maze of the Anafiotika quarter.

Emerging at Monastiraki station you are confronted with all of Athens' chaos and charm, grit and ancient splendour – the Acropolis looming above, souvlaki aromas wafting from Mitropoleos, the bustling flea market and seemingly endless construction work. New and spruced-up cafés and restaurants along Adrianou have livened up the area, while Plateia Monastirakiou (Monastiraki Sq) has had a major facelift.

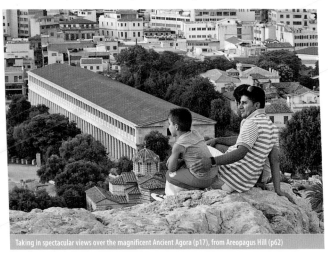

Taking in spectacular views over the magnificent Ancient Agora (p17), from Areopagus Hill (p62)

PLAKA & MONASTIRAKI

◎ SEE
Agios Nikolaos Rangavas **1** F5
Agios Symeon....................**2** E5
Ancient Agora...................**3** A4
Areopagus Hill.................**4** B5
Athens Archaeological
  Service.........................**5** C3
Athens Cathedral **6** F2
Centre of Folk Art &
  Tradition.....................**7** G5
Church of Kapnikarea.....**8** E1
Church of
  Metamorphosis...........**9** H4
Church of the Holy
  Apostles of Solakis....**10** B3
Hadrian's Library..........**11** C2
Hellenic Children's
  Museum.....................**12** G5
Jewish Museum............**13** H4
Kanellopoulos
  Museum.....................**14** C4
Little Metropolis **15** F2
Lysikrates Monument ..**16** F6
Museum of Children's
  Art.............................**17** H4
Museum of Greek Folk
  Art.............................**18** H5
Museum of Greek Folk
  Art: Man & Tools........**19** C4
Museum of Greek Popular
  Instruments **20** E3
Museum of Traditional
  Greek Ceramics **21** C2

Panagia Grigoroussa,
  Taxiarhon &
  Fanouriou..................**22** C3
Roman Agora.................**23** D3
Tower of the Winds **24** D3
Turkish Baths................**25** E4

🛍 SHOP
Amorgos.......................**26** H4
Archipelagos.................**27** F5
Byzantino......................**28** F4
Carnaby St....................**29** C1
Centre of Hellenic
  Tradition....................**30** D2
Compendium................**31** H4
Eleftheroudakis...........**32** H3
Fine Wine.....................**33** G6
Koukos.........................**34** G4
Martinos.......................**35** D2
Melissinos Art...............**36** C1
Mesogaia......................**37** H5
Monastiraki Flea
  Market.......................**38** B2
Mythos.........................**39** H4
Spiliopoulos.................**40** C2
Thelgitron **41** F5

🍴 EAT
Amalthia......................**42** F4
Café Avyssinia **43** B1
Glykis..........................**44** G5
Kalipateira...................**45** A1

Klepsidra **46** D4
Kostas..........................**47** F4
Nama...........................**48** A2
O Damigos
  Bakaliarika................**49** G5
Ouzou Melathron **50** B1
Palia Taverna Tou
  Psara.........................**51** E4
Platanos **52** E3
Thanasis **53** D2
To Kafeneio..................**54** F5

▶ DRINK
Brettos.........................**55** G5
Dioskouri **56** C2
James Joyce..................**57** A1
Kinky............................**58** D1
Magaze........................**59** D1
Melina **60** E4
Tristrato.......................**61** G5

★ PLAY
Cine Paris.....................**62** G5
Perivoli Tou Ouranou....**63** G6
Zygos...........................**64** G5

Please see over for map

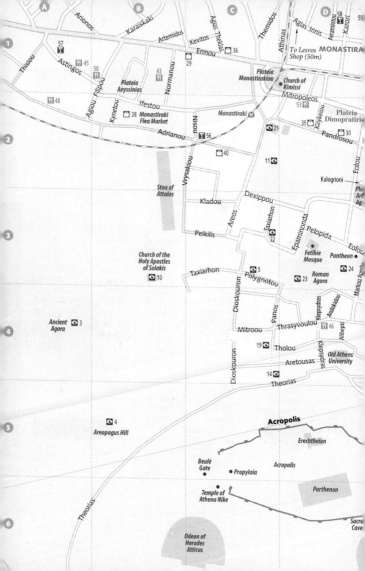

MONASTIRA

To Lesvos
Shop (50m)

Plateia
Monastirakiou

Church of
Kimissi

Mitropoleos

Plateia
Dimopratirie

Monastiraki

Plateia
Avyssinias

Ifestou

Monastiraki
Flea Market

Adrianou

Pandrosou

Kalogrioni

Stoa of
Attalos

Kladou

Dexippou

Pelopida

Peikilis

Church of the
Holy Apostles
of Solakis

Taxiarhon

Polygnotou

Fetihie
Mosque

Pantheon

Roman
Agora

Ancient
Agora

Mitroou

Thrasyvoulou

Tholou

Old Athens
University

Aretousas

Theorias

Areopagus Hill

Acropolis

Erechtheion

Beulé
Gate

Propylaia

Acropolis

Temple of
Athena Nike

Parthenon

Theorias

Odeon of
Herodes
Atticus

Sacre
Cave

👁 SEE

👁 ANCIENT AGORA

☎ 210 321 0185; entrances on Adrianou, Theorias & Vrysakiou, Monastiraki; admission €4 (free with Acropolis pass); ⏱ 8am-7pm Tue-Sun, 11am-7pm Mon Apr-Oct, 8am-5pm Nov-Mar; Ⓜ Monastiraki or Thisio

Athens' ancient marketplace is a fascinating site to explore. It's here you'll find the superb Temple of Hephaestus, Agora Museum and the Byzantine Church of the Holy Apostles of Solakis (p66). See also p17 for more information.

Church of the Holy Apostles of Solakis (p17)

👁 AREOPAGUS HILL

Admission free; Plaka; Ⓜ Monastiraki

Diagonally opposite the main Acropolis entrance, you'll see new stairs leading up to the hallowed rocky spur of Areopagus Hill (the worn steps got too dangerous for most). Once the meeting place for the supreme council, contemplative tourists and romantics are found there at all hours enjoying superb views over the Ancient Agora.

👁 ATHENS CATHEDRAL & LITTLE METROPOLIS

☎ 210 322 1308; Plateia Mitropoleos, Monastiraki; ⏱ 7am-7pm, Sun Mass 6.30am; Ⓜ Monastiraki

The ornate 1862 Athens Cathedral on Plateia Mitropoleos (Mitropoleos Sq) is the seat of the archbishop of the Greek Orthodox Church of Athens. However, far more significant, both historically and architecturally, is the small 12th-century church next to the cathedral, known as the Little Metropolis. Its official double-barrelled name – it's dedicated to two saints – is Church of Panagia Gorgeopikoos (Virgin Swift to Hear) and Agios Eleftherios. The cruciform-style marble church was built on the ruins of an ancient temple and made using reliefs and pieces of ancient and early-Christian monuments.

◉ CENTRE OF FOLK ART & TRADITION

☎ 210 324 3972; Hatzimihali Agelikis 6, Plaka; admission free; ⏱ 9am-1pm & 5-9pm Tue-Fri, 9am-1pm Sat & Sun; Ⓜ Akropoli or Syntagma

The 1920s mansion of folklorist Angeliki Hatzimichalis recreates the traditional pastoral life, including an old kitchen and chapel. Exhibits include regional costumes, embroideries, weaving machines, ceramic vases and family portraits. At the time of writing, it was closed for refurbishment.

◉ CHURCH OF KAPNIKAREA

☎ 210 322 4462; Kapnikareas (cnr Ermou), Monastiraki; ⏱ 8am-1pm Mon, Wed & Sat, 8am-1pm & 4-8pm Tue, Thu & Fri, 8-11.30am Sun; Ⓜ Monastiraki

The 13-century Byzantine Church of Kapnikarea

TOWER OF THE WINDS

The well-preserved octagonal **Tower of the Winds**, on the site of the Roman Agora (p66), was built about 150–125 BC by the Syrian astronomer Andronicus. It's an ingenious construction, functioning as a sundial, weather vane, water clock and compass. Made of Pentelic marble, it had a bronze triton that revolved on top of the tower as a weather vane, and reliefs of eight wind figures on each side depicting the wind patterns. Beneath each of the reliefs are the faint markings of sundials. It was converted to a church, later used for dervishes under Ottoman rule.

Right in the middle of the Ermou shopping mall is the tiny 13th-century Byzantine Church of Kapnikarea. The cruciform-style domed church was nearly destroyed to make way for progress, but was saved and restored by Athens University.

◉ HADRIAN'S LIBRARY

Areos, Monastiraki; Ⓜ Monastiraki

Once the most luxurious public building in the city, Hadrian's library was erected around AD 132. It had an internal courtyard and pool and was bordered by 100 columns. The building was destroyed in AD 267 during the Herulian invasion. The remains of Megali Panagia, believed to be the oldest Christian church in Athens, can be seen in the garden, includ-

LYSIKRATES MONUMENT

The Lysikrates Monument (Tripodon, Plaka; M Acropoli), on one of Athens' oldest streets, stands as one of the city's most significant ancient monuments. It was erected in 335–334 BC by Lysicrates, a choragus (sponsor) of drama contests, to display the bronze tripod trophies. The well-preserved circular building has six Corinthian columns and a frieze showing scenes from Dionysos' life. In 1669 it was incorporated into a Capuchin monastery and turned into a library, where Lord Byron allegedly wrote part of *Childe Harold's Pilgrimage*.

ing parts of the mosaic floor. During the Ottoman period it was a bazaar.

⊙ HELLENIC CHILDREN'S MUSEUM

☎ 210 331 2995; www.hcm.gr; Kydathineon 14, Plaka; admission free; ⏱ 10am-2pm Tue-Fri, 10am-3pm Sat & Sun, closed Jul & Aug; M Syntagma

Activities at this interactive centre encourage children's development and engage the imagination, including a popular chocolate-making session. Exhibits are in Greek only; some activities are suitable for non-Greek speakers and most staff speak English.

⊙ JEWISH MUSEUM

☎ 210 322 5582; www.jewishmuseum.gr; Nikis 39, Plaka; adult/child €5/3; ⏱ 9am-2.30pm Mon-Fri, 10am-2pm Sun; M Syntagma

This museum traces the history of the Jewish community in Greece from the 3rd century BC, with an impressive collection of religious and historical artefacts, documents, folk art and costumes. Nearly 90% of Greece's Jews, most from Thessaloniki, were killed during the Holocaust.

⊙ KANELLOPOULOS MUSEUM

☎ 210 321 2313; Theorias 12 (cnr Panos), Monastiraki; ⏱ 8.30am-3pm Tue-Sun; M Monastiraki

The imposing 1884 mansion on the northern slope of the Acropolis houses the Kanellopoulos family's extensive collection, donated to the state in 1976. After a major refurbishment and expansion, it was due to open in late 2008. The collection includes jewellery, clay-and-stone vases and figurines, weapons, Byzantine icons, bronzes and objets d'art dating from every period of Greek history.

⊙ MUSEUM OF GREEK CHILDREN'S ART

☎ 210 331 2621; www.childrensartmuseum.gr; Kodrou 9, Plaka; adult/child €2/free; ⏱ 10am-2pm Tue-Sat, 11am-2pm Sun Sep-Jul, closed Aug; M Syntagma

Founded to cultivate a love of art and creative development, this museum is one of the few of its kind in the world. There are exhibitions of young artists' work and workshops for children.

 MUSEUM OF GREEK FOLK ART

☎ 210 322 9031; www.culture.gr; Kydathineon 17, Plaka; admission €2; ☾ 9am-2pm Tue-Sun; Ⓜ Syntagma

This fine state-owned museum has examples of folk art from 1650 to the present, including elaborate embroidery, weaving, costumes, shadow-theatre puppets and silverwork. The 1st floor has fine wall murals by renowned naive artist Theophilos Hatzimichail, and a temporary exhibition gallery.

MUSEUM OF GREEK FOLK ART: MAN & TOOLS

☎ 210 321 4972; www.culture.gr; Panos 22, Plaka; admission €2; ☾ 9am-2.30pm Tue-Sun; Ⓜ Syntagma

As the name suggests, this museum takes a historical journey through a well-displayed collection of tools and machinery, spread out in a warren of small rooms in a stately early 19th-century Plaka house.

MUSEUM OF GREEK POPULAR INSTRUMENTS

☎ 210 325 0198; www.culture.gr; Diogenous 1-3, Plaka; admission free; ☾ 10am-2pm Tue & Thu-Sun, noon-6pm Wed; Ⓜ Monastiraki

More than 1200 folk instruments dating from the 18th century are exhibited over three floors, with

Costumes on display at the Museum of Greek Folk Art

headphones for visitors to listen to the sounds of the *gaida* (Greek goatskin bagpipes) and Byzantine mandolins, among others. Musical performances are held in the lovely garden in summer.

MUSEUM OF TRADITIONAL GREEK CERAMICS

☎ 210 324 2066; Areos 1, Monastiraki; admission €2; ✆ 9am-2.30pm Mon & Wed-Sun; Ⓜ Monastiraki

The Mosque of Tzistarakis (built in 1759) is one of few surviving examples of a *tzami* (mosque) in Athens. It houses this annexe of the Museum of Greek Folk Art and features pottery and hand-painted ceramics from the early 20th century.

ROMAN AGORA

☎ 210 324 5220; www.culture.gr; cnr Eolou & Pelopida, Plaka; admission €2 (free with Acropolis pass); ✆ 8am-7pm Apr-Oct, 8am-5pm Nov-Mar; Ⓜ Monastiraki

The city's civic centre under Roman rule was moved to this partly excavated site, where you can see the foundations of several structures, including a 1st-century, 68-seat public latrine to the right of the entry, and a propylon (entrance) at the southeastern corner. The well-preserved Gate of Athena Archegetis, flanked by four Doric columns, was erected in the 1st century AD and financed by Julius Caesar. The

---

PLAKA'S BYZANTINE CHURCHES

One of the oldest Byzantine churches in Athens (built around AD 1000) is the **Church of the Holy Apostles of Solakis**, on the site of the Ancient Agora (p62). During the period of Ottoman rule it underwent many changes, but was restored in the 1950s. It has frescoes transferred from a demolished church.

The 11th-century **Agios Nikolaos Rangavas** (☎ 210 322 8193; Prytaniou 1, cnr Epiharmou, Plaka; ✆ 8am-noon & 5-8pm; Ⓜ Monastiraki) was part of the palace of the Rangava family, which included Michael I, emperor of Byzantium. The church bell was the first installed in Athens after liberation from the Turks (who banned them) and was the first to ring in 1833 to announce the freedom of Athens.

Built in 1031, **Sotira Lykodimou** (Map pp40-1, F4; Filellinon, near Kydathineon, Plaka; ☎ 7am-10am; Ⓜ Monastiraki) is the largest medieval structure (and only octagonal Byzantine church) in Athens, and has served as the Russian Orthodox Church since 1847.

Every Saturday afternoon, worshippers arrive at **Panagia Grigoroussa, Taxiarhon & Fanouriou** (cnr Taxiarhon & Epaminonda, near Adrianou, Plaka; ✆ 5.45pm Apr-Oct, 4.45pm Nov-Mar; Ⓜ Monastiraki) for a special service to get their *fanouropita* (spiced raisin cake) blessed before sharing it with passers-by. The cake is supposed to help you find something lost or someone you may be seeking.

Fethiye Djami mosque on the northern side of the Agora is one of the city's few surviving reminders of Ottoman times. Predating the Agora is the fascinating Tower of the Winds (p63).

TURKISH BATHS

☎ 210 324 4340; Kyristou 8, Monastiraki; admission €2; ◷ 9am-2.30pm Tue-Sun; Ⓜ Monastiraki

The only surviving public bathhouse in Athens is one of the few remnants of the Ottoman period. The refurbished 17th-century bathhouse of Abit Efendi gives some insight into the rituals of the era, when bathhouses were an important meeting point.

SHOP

AMORGOS Souvenirs

☎ 210 324 3836; Kodrou 3, Plaka; ◷ 11am-3pm & 6-8pm Mon-Fri; Ⓜ Syntagma

A charming store crammed with authentic Greek folk art, trinkets, ceramics, embroideries and collectables, plus wood-carved furniture and items made by owner Kostas Kaitatzis, whose wife Rena runs the store.

ARCHIPELAGOS Jewellery

☎ 210 323 1321; Adrianou 142, Plaka; ◷ 10am-9pm, later in summer; Ⓜ Monastiraki

Unique contemporary pieces in silver and gold for jewellery lovers with moderate budgets. There are also interesting ceramics and trinkets, including fine silver bookmarks.

BYZANTINO Jewellery

☎ 210 324 6605; Adrianou 120, Plaka; Ⓜ Monastiraki

One of the best of the myriad stores in Plaka selling gold in ancient and Byzantine motifs; the jewellery here is handcrafted by the owners.

CARNABY ST Street Wear

☎ 210 331 5333; Ermou 99 (cnr Normanou), Monastiraki; Ⓜ Monastiraki

Designer streetwear, including London labels, as well as a range of funky T-shirts from Greek brand Fingerprint in this new cluster of trendy clothing stores.

CENTRE OF HELLENIC TRADITION Souvenirs & Ceramics

☎ 210 321 3023; Pandrosou 36 (or Mitropoleos 59), Monastiraki; ◷ 9am-8pm Mar-Nov, 9am-7pm Dec-Feb; Ⓜ Monastiraki

Upstairs in this arcade are great examples of traditional ceramics, sculptures, woodcarvings, paintings and folk art from prominent Greek artists. The quaint café-ouzerie has Acropolis views, and there's an art gallery upstairs.

🏠 COMPENDIUM *Books*
☎ 210 322 1248; Navarhou Nikodimou 5 (cnr Nikis), Plaka; Ⓜ Syntagma
A good selection of new and used books, with popular and quality literature, travel guides and books on Greece.

🏠 ELEFTHEROUDAKIS *Books & Music*
☎ 210 323 1401; Nikis 20, Plaka; ☺ 9am-9pm Mon-Fri, 9am-6pm Sat; Ⓜ Syntagma
Not as big as its megastore parent in Syntagma (p45), the Plaka branch has a range of books on Greece, travel guides, and Greek and English literature.

🏠 FINE WINE *Wine*
☎ 210 323 0350; Lysikratous 3,Plaka; Ⓜ Syntagma
This delightful, refurbished old store has a great selection of fine Greek wines and spirits, including gift packs. The friendly and knowledgeable owners can guide you through Greece's unique grape varieties.

🏠 KOUKOS *Souvenirs*
☎ 210 322 2740; Navarhou Nikodimou 21, Plaka; Ⓜ Syntagma
A great collection of Italian pewter picture frames, platters, jugs, replicas of Greek monk's hip flasks and other items. Koukos also stocks a range of antique ceramics and original silver handcrafted jewellery.

🏠 MARTINOS *Antiques*
☎ 210 321 2414; www.martinosart.gr; Pandrosou 50, Monastiraki; Ⓜ Monastiraki
This Monastiraki landmark opened in 1890 and has an excellent selection of Greek and European antiques and collectables, including painted dowry chests, icons, coins, glassware, porcelain and furniture.

🏠 MELISSINOS ART *Leather Sandals*
☎ 210 321 9247; www.melissinos-poet .com; Agias Theklas 2, Monastiraki; Ⓜ Monastiraki
Athens' famous sandal-maker and poet, septuagenarian Stavros Melissinos, has pretty much handed the reins to artist son Pantelis, who continues making classic leather sandals modelled on ancient styles, and adds his own touch to more than 32 designs.

🏠 MESOGAIA *Food & Wine*
☎ 210 322 9146; Nikis 52 (cnr Kydathineon), Plaka; ☺ 9am-5pm Mon & Wed, 9am-9pm Tue, Thu & Fri, 9am-4pm Sat Mar-Nov, also 10am-3pm Sun Dec-Jan; Ⓜ Syntagma
Foodies will love the range of traditional products from all over

Greece, including cheeses, yoghurts and biscuits for immediate consumption or take-home jars of thyme honey with walnuts, olive oil, *pasteli* (honey and sesame sweets) and other edible treats.

MONASTIRAKI FLEA MARKET *Market*

Adrianou, Ifestou & Plateia Avyssinias, Monastiraki; antique stalls 8am-3pm, rest 8am-late; M Monastiraki
Wandering through Athens' flea market is an eclectic shopping experience. This is the place to stumble on anything from that rare vinyl record, military boots, old books, antiques, to furniture and collectables. It's in its element on Sundays, when vendors line up along Adrianou, the cafés and restaurants reach bursting point and the area takes on a festive atmosphere. Having outgrown its capacity, more mainstream traders have moved to the big Sunday flea market (p81) in Thisio.

MYTHOS
Jewellery & Accessories
☎ 210 324 9160; Kydathineon 6, Plaka; 10am-10.30pm Apr-Oct, 10am-9pm Nov-Mar; M Syntagma
This tiny store at the fringes of Plaka's tourist drag has a fine selection of interesting and reasonably priced jewellery, artwork, crafts and other goodies that make great small gifts.

Shoppers browsing the vast range of goods on offer at the Monastiraki flea market

🛍 **SPILIOPOULOS** *Shoes & Bags*
☎ 210 321 9096; Adrianou 50, Plaka; Ⓜ Monastiraki
More spacious and less chaotic than the original Ermou store in Syntagma (p46), this is the place to try to nab bargain designer and imported shoes, handbags and clothing.

🏛 **THELGITRON** *Jewellery*
☎ 210 324 4475; Adrianou 130, Plaka; Ⓜ Syntagma
In the tiny workshop of Konstantinos Gouveris you'll find some unique contemporary designs that stand out from the usual Plaka tourist offerings. He mostly works in silver.

🍴 EAT

🍴 **AMALTHIA** *Crêperie* €
Tripodon 16, Plaka; Ⓜ Akropoli
On one of the oldest streets in Greece, the ancient Street of Tripods, this delightful old-style café with marble tables specialises in crepes, but also does excellent traditional sweets, including a delicious *galaktoboureko* (custard slice).

🍴 **CAFÉ AVYSSINIA**
Mezedhopoleio €€
☎ 210 321 7047; Plateia Avyssinias, Monastiraki; ⏱ 11am-late Tue-Sat, 11am-7pm Sun, closed mid Jul–Aug; Ⓜ Monastiraki

In the heart of charmingly grungy Plateias Avyssinias (Avyssinias Sq), this atmospheric place has excellent mezedhes, such as the delicious marinated *gavros* (anchovies). Occasional live music and a bit of a cult following. Best enjoyed on weekends for a late lunch.

🍴 **GLYKIS** *Mezedhopoleio* €
☎ 210 322 3925; Angelou Geronta 2, Plaka; ⏱ 10am-late; Ⓜ Syntagma
In a quiet corner of Plaka, this casual place with a leafy courtyard is frequented by students and locals. It has a tasty selection of mezedhes, including traditional dishes such as *briam* (vegetable casserole dish in tomato sauce) and cuttlefish in wine.

🍴 **KALIPATEIRA**
Mezedhopoleio €
☎ 210 321 4152; Astingos 8, Monastiraki; Ⓜ Monastiraki
In a neoclassic building overlooking an archaeological dig, young Athenians gather for long sessions over carafes of ouzo, snacking on one of the *pikilies* (mixed mezedhes). There are acoustic *rembetika* (Greek blues) and Cretan live music Thursday to Sunday.

🍴 **KLEPSYDRA** *Café* €
☎ 210 321 4152; Klepsydras; Monastiraki; Ⓜ Monastiraki

Tucked away in a delightfully quiet spot under the Acropolis, with shady outdoor tables and friendly service, Klepsydra is a favourite with locals and an ideal rest spot after serious sightseeing; there's a small selection of snacks, such as *spanakopites* (spinach pies).

🍴 KOSTAS *Souvlaki* €
☎ 210 322 8502; Adrianou 116, Plaka; ⏱ 8am-2.30pm Mon-Fri; Ⓜ Monastiraki
You'll often see people hanging around outside this tiny hole-in-the-wall, where young Kosta continues his grandfather's tradition, churning out tasty pork souvlaki with his unique garnish. He often sells out early.

🍴 NAMA *Café-restaurant* €€
☎ 210 321 1233; Adrianou 29; Monastiraki; Ⓜ Monastiraki
Arguably the most amazing toilets in Athens, with glass floors exposing the ancient ruins underfoot, this new arrival has a sleek modern design and menu to match.

🍴 O DAMIGOS BAKALIARIKA *Taverna* €
☎ 210 322 5084; Kydathineon 41, Plaka; ⏱ dinner (closed Jun-Aug); Ⓜ Syntagma
Reputedly Plaka's oldest taverna, this basement eatery features in many old Greek movies. It's a lively winter place for traditional

Greek fare; just mind your step on the way in. The house speciality is *bakaliaro* (salty cod fried in batter), served with a lethal garlic dip.

🍴 OUZOU MELATHRON *Modern Greek* €€
☎ 210 324 0716; Agiou Filipou 10 (cnr Astingos), Monastiraki; ⏱ lunch & dinner; Ⓜ Monastiraki
This successful Thessaloniki restaurant is gimmicky, with overly complicated and oversized menus, but the food does not disappoint. Friendly service and a range of creative mezedhes make it one of the better offerings in the area.

🍴 PALIA TAVERNA TOU PSARA *Seafood Taverna* €€
☎ 210 321 8733; Erehtheos 16 (cnr Erotokritou), Plaka; ⏱ 10am-1am; Ⓜ Monastiraki
One of the older and well-regarded tavernas in Plaka, known for its seafood mezedhes, this atmospheric place in a renovated 1898 house has pleasant shaded courtyard and tables on the charming Plaka street.

🍴 PLATANOS *Taverna* €
☎ 210 322 0666; Diogenous 4, Plaka; ⏱ lunch & dinner Mon-Sat; Ⓜ Monastiraki
This village-style taverna with tables under the giant plane tree

Maria Panagiotopoulou
Publicist, Athens Festival (p27)

Athens festival highlight The Herodion (Odeon of Herodes Atticus; p57) is a magical experience. International artists love to play there, it's very prestigious. **Walks around Athens** The promenade is wonderful. Start from Akropol metro (Map p51, C2, D2) and walk to the cafés in Thisio (p85) and Monastirak (opposite). It's like a walk in history. **Regular drinking hole** Skoufaki (p121) in Kolonaki was the first to open on that street and still has a special atmosphere and its regulars. **Modern Greek food** Mani Mani (p56); food is lovely, nice atmosphere, polite service. **Meatlovers** To Steki Tou Ilia (p84) in Thisio, for grilled lamb chops. **Athens lowdown** Athens is not the nicest city, but it has very nice parts. It's friendly, the nightlife is exceptional. You can always find nice bars and people just having a drink at 3am. You can also have surprises, meet a group of people, go to another bar and end up somewhere else.

in the courtyard is popular among Greeks and tourists. It serves delicious home-style fare, such as oven-baked potatoes, lamb fricassee and beef with quince and summer greens.

THANASIS *Souvlaki* €

☎ 210 324 4705; Mitropoleos 69, Monastiraki; ☽ 8.30am-2.30am Ⓜ Monastiraki

In the heart of Athens' souvlaki hub, at the end of Mitropoleos, Thanasis is known for its kebabs on pitta with grilled tomato and onions. Live music, wafting grill aromas and constant crowds give the area an almost permanently festive air.

TO KAFENEIO
Mezedhopoleio €€

☎ 210 324 6916; Epiharmou 1 (cnr Tripodon), Plaka,; ☽ lunch & dinner; Ⓜ Akropoli

A cosy place with stone walls and exposed timber ceilings, Kafeneio has an interesting assortment of regional mezedhes, including Cretan cheese pies and aubergine croquettes.

DRINK
BRETTOS *Bar*

☎ 210 323 2110; Kydathineon 41, Plaka; ☽ 10am-midnight; Ⓜ Syntagma

A Plaka landmark, this quaint bar has a stunning backlit wall of

Bar flies enjoying a pint or two at the Irish pub, James Joyce (p75)

coloured bottles, old wine barrels and an authentic old-fashioned character. It's a quiet spot for a night- (or day-) cap, with a tempting range of homemade brews to imbibe or take away.

▼ DIOSKOURI *Café*
☎ 210 325 3333; Adrianou 37, Plaka; Ⓜ Monastiraki

A landmark café in Plaka sitting virtually over the railway line, the tables under a huge plane tree give it a traditional village feel. It's popular with students for mezedhes and ouzo.

▼ JAMES JOYCE *Pub*
☎ 210 323 5055; Astingos 12, Monastiraki; Ⓜ Monastiraki

With freeflowing Guinness and tasty burgers and pub food, this rather incongruous Irish pub has settled comfortably into a reviving pocket of old Athens.

▼ KINKY *Bar*
☎ 210 321 0355; Avramiotou 6-8, Monastiraki; ☽ 9pm-late; Ⓜ Monastiraki

Kinky is one of the original trendy breed of small, funky bars hidden in obscure alleys in downtown Athens. You'll spot patrons lounging on the ornate bed outside.

▼ MAGAZE *Café-bar*
☎ 210 324 3740; Eolou 33, Monastiraki; ☽ 10am-late; Ⓜ Monastiraki

With tables on the pedestrian strip near Plateia Agias Irinis looking up to the Acropolis, this gay-friendly place is popular day and night. If you're lost you can check out the large-scale Athens map on the wall.

▼ MELINA *Café*
☎ 210 324 6501; Lyssiou 22, Plaka; ☽ noon-late; Ⓜ Monastiraki

This quaint old-world-style café is decorated with memorabilia and photographs celebrating Greece's legendary actress and politician, the late Melina Mercouri.

▼ TRISTRATO *Café*
☎ 210 324 4472; cnr Angelou Geronta & Dedalou, Plaka, ☽ 10am-1am; Ⓜ Syntagma

This gem off Plaka's busy square with a wonderful traditional ambience specialises in milk-based desserts, herbal and mountain teas, milkshakes, and makes a wicked hot chocolate with a dash of cognac.

★ PLAY

▣ CINE PARIS *Outdoor Cinema*
☎ 210 322 2071; Kydathineon 22, Plaka; tickets €8; Ⓜ Syntagma

A magical place to see a movie, this traditional old rooftop cinema in Plaka has great views of the Acropolis from some seats.

⭐ PERIVOLI TOU OURANOU
Music Taverna

☎ 210 323 5517; Lysikratous 19, Plaka; ☼ 9pm-late Thu-Sun; Ⓜ Akropoli, Syntagma

A favourite Plaka music haunt in a rustic old-style venue where you can have dinner and listen to authentic *laïka* (urban popular music) and *rembetika* by leading exponents.

⭐ ZYGOS *Live Music*

☎ 210 324 1610; Kydathineon 22, Plaka; ☼ 11pm-3am Thu-Sat; 9pm-1am Sun Nov-Apr; Ⓜ Syntagma

One of the few surviving music venues in Plaka, Zygos hosts *entehno* (quality) artists. The entry price covers a drink and standing room only. Tables have pricey minimum alcohol charges.

>PSYRRI, THISIO & KERAMIKOS

Once touted as the 'Soho' of Athens, Psyrri led the urban revival. Behind its dilapidated façade is a lively quarter where restaurants, bars, theatres and clubs coexist with an offbeat mix of warehouse conversions, restored neoclassical houses, galleries, fashion ateliers, quirky stores and workshops. Renowned for merry Sunday afternoons in its live-music tavernas, Psyrri comes alive after dusk, though lately it's becoming saturated with mainstream crowds, while its outer pockets are decidedly seedy.

Thisio blossomed after cars were banished to make way for the pedestrian promenade. Young Athenians have claimed the café precinct that emerged under the Acropolis, while the free concerts and public events make Thisio a thriving social hub.

Keramikos is also being transformed with the pedestrianisation of Ermou, where the lively Sunday flea market takes place opposite the archaeological site. With restaurants and bars sprouting in its quiet residential quarter, Keramikos is an emerging hotspot.

PSYRRI, THISIO & KERAMIKOS

◉ SEE
A.Antonopoulou.Art	1	E2
Agios Athanasios Church	2	C3
Bernier/Eliades Gallery	3	C3
Dipylon Gate	(see 10)	
Herakleidon	4	C4
Islamic Art Museum	5	D2
Keramikos	6	C2
Keramikos Museum	7	B3
Melina Mercouri Cultural Centre	8	B3
Museum of Traditional Pottery	9	D2
Sacred Gate	10	C2

◉ SHOP
Christoforos Kotentos	11	E1
Epidemic	12	E2
Mofu	13	E2
Shop	14	E3
Sunday Flea Market	15	A3
Yeshop Inhouse	16	E2

🍴 EAT
Athiri	17	B1
Avalon	18	D2
Filistron	19	D5
Ikonomou	20	A7
Ivis	21	E3
Kouzina	22	D2
Kuzina	23	D3
Nikitas	24	E2
Oineas	25	E2
Pil Poul	26	C3
Therapeftirio	27	A7
To Steki Tou Ilia	28	C3
Varoulko	29	C1

🍸 DRINK
Alekos' Island	30	D2
Apsenti	31	B4
Cantina Social	32	D3
Peonia Herbs	33	C3
Soul	34	E1
Stavlos	35	C4

⭐ PLAY
Bios	36	C2
Dora Stratou Dance Theatre	37	B8
El Pecado	38	D2
Envy	39	F2
Thirio	40	E2
Thission	41	D5
Zefyros	42	A7

Please see over for map

NEIGHBOURHOODS

SEE

A.ANTONOPOULOU.ART

☎ 210 321 4994; 4th fl, Aristofanous 20, Psyrri; ⏲ 2-9pm Tue-Fri, noon-4pm Sat (closed mid-Jul–late Aug); Ⓜ Monastiraki

One of the original galleries to open in Psyrri's warehouses, this impressive art space hosts a range of exhibitions of contemporary and international art, including installations, video art and photography by emerging Greek artists.

BERNIER/ELIADES GALLERY

☎ 210 341 3936; www.bernier-eliades .gr; Eptahalkou 11, Thisio; ⏲ 10.30am-8pm Tue-Fri, noon-4pm Sat; Ⓜ Thisio

This well-established gallery showcases prominent Greek artists and an impressive list of international artists, from abstract American impressionists to British pop.

HERAKLEIDON

☎ 210 346 1981; www.herakleidon-art .gr; Iraklidon 16, Thisio; admission €6; ⏲ 1-9pm, closed mid-Aug; Ⓜ Thisio; ♿

Housed in a beautifully refurbished neoclassical building

PSYRRI, THISIO & KERAMIKOS

The Herakleidon houses one of the world's largest private MC Escher collections

PSYRRI, THISIO & KERAMIKOS

THEMISTOCLEAN WALL
In the Keramikos site you can see the longest and best-preserved section of the 479 BC Themistoclean wall (C2), a 6.5km-long structure built around Athens to protect the city. The wall was reinforced with towers and had 15 gates leading to other parts of Attica and Piraeus. You can see a part of the wall under the Islamic Art Museum (below) and various parts of the city, while the remains of one of the gates is on display opposite and underneath the National Bank of Greece building on Eolou (Map p95, E2).

among the busy café strip in Thisio, this private museum has one of the world's biggest collections of MC Escher and also hosts temporary exhibitions. There's a great little café in the courtyard, and a gift shop.

☑ ISLAMIC ART MUSEUM
☎ 210 325 1311; www.benaki.gr; Agion Asomaton 22 (cnr Dipylou), Keramikos; adult/child €5/3; ☒ 9am-3pm Tue & Thu-Sun, 9am-9pm Wed; Ⓜ Thisio; ♿
The Benaki Museum's celebrated collection of Islamic art is one of the finest in the world. This stately neoclassical complex of buildings exhibits more than 8000 items covering the 12th to 19th centuries, including weavings, carvings, prayer carpets,

tiles, ceramics and a 17th-century reception room from a Cairo mansion.

☑ KERAMIKOS
☎ 210 346 3552; www.culture.gr; Ermou 148, Keramikos; admission €2 (free with Acropolis pass); ☒ 8am-7pm Apr-Oct, 11am-7.30pm Mon, 8am-5pm Nov-Mar; Ⓜ Thisio
The often-missed Keramikos site, the ancient cemetery of Athens, is one of the most peaceful open spaces in the city. See p22 for further details.

☑ MELINA MERCOURI CULTURAL CENTRE
☎ 210 345 2150; Iraklidon 66 (cnr Thessalonikis); admission free; ☒ 9am-1pm & 5-9pm Mon-Fri; Ⓜ Thisio; ♿
The landmark Poulopoulou hat factory hosts free photographic and cultural exhibitions. Its permanent exhibition is an impressive re-creation of an Athenian street in 1900, with houses, shops and a *kafeneio* (coffee house), while the basement houses the Haridimos shadow-puppet museum.

☑ MUSEUM OF TRADITIONAL POTTERY
☎ 210 331 8491; Melidoni 4-6, Keramikos; admission €3; ☒ 9-3pm Mon-Fri, 10am-2pm Sat Ⓜ Thisio
This small museum in a lovely neoclassical building around

the corner from the Keramikos site is dedicated to the history of (relatively) contemporary Greek pottery, exhibiting a selection from the museum's 4500-plus collection. There's a reconstruction of a traditional potter's workshop. The centre holds periodic exhibitions.

 # SHOP

CHRISTOFOROS KOTENTOS
Fashion Designer
☎ 210 325 5156; www.christoforoskotentos.com; Sahtouri 3, Psyrri; ⏱ 10am-6pm; Ⓜ Monastiraki
You'll have to be buzzed up to the 4th-floor atelier and workshop of this hot local designer, whose evening and casual clothing range is sold in Milan, New York and Tokyo. Designer Vasso Consola is also based in the same warehouse.

EPIDEMIC *Street Wear*
☎ 210 321 1390; Agion Anargyron 5, Psyrri; ⏱ 11am-9pm Mon-Fri, 10am-8pm Sat, 1-8pm Sun; Ⓜ Monastiraki
A funky gallery-like store with designer street-wear, club wear and loads of accessories with attitude for men and women.

MOFU *Interior Design*
☎ 210 331 9220; Sarri 28, Psyrri; Ⓜ Thisio
Retro fans will adore the eclectic range of largely '50s, '60s and '70s furniture, lamps and odd designer collectables in this friendly store. It's happy to arrange shipping if you just have to have that piece.

SHOP *Fashion*
☎ 210 321 6694; Ermou 112a, Psyrri; Ⓜ Thisio
Located at the gritty end of Ermou, this store has two levels full of trendy international designer street wear brands such as Energie, Carhart and Miss Sixty for the young and young at heart.

YESHOP INHOUSE
Fashion Designer
☎ 210 331 2622; www.yiorgoselefth eriades.gr; Agion Anargyron 13, Psyrri; ⏱ noon-8pm Tue, Thu & Fri; noon-6pm Wed & Sat; Ⓜ Monastiraki
The bright 1st-floor atelier of local designer Yiorgos Eleftheriades showcases his latest edgy men's and women's urban clothing and accessories range.

SUNDAY FLEA MARKET
The big **Sunday flea market** (⏱ 6am-2pm Sun; Ⓜ Thisio) takes place on Ermou starting at the entrance to Keramikos all the way to Thisio Park. Traders peddle their motley wares, while bargain-hunters scour through the aisles in search of that special something. This is the place to test your haggling skills.

🍴 EAT

🍴 ATHIRI *Modern Greek* €€

☎ 210 346 2983; Plateon 15, Keramikos; 🕑 closed Monday; Ⓜ Thisio

Athiri's lovely garden courtyard is a verdant surprise in this pocket of Keramikos, while the small but innovative menu playing on Greek regional classics is well executed. Try Santorini fava and the hearty beef stew with *myzithra* (sheep's-milk cheese) and handmade pasta from Karpathos.

🍴 AVALON *Bar-restaurant* €€

☎ 210 331 0572; Leokoriou 20 (cnr Sarri), Psyrri; 🕑 lunch & dinner Sun, dinner Tue-Sat Ⓜ Monastiraki or Thisio

The atmosphere is part-Greek part-medieval, but the mussels are the main attraction, cooked with almost any spice and sauce you can imagine. The pleasant court-yard opens its roof in summer.

🍴 FILISTRON *Mezedhopoleio* €€

☎ 210 346 7554; Apostolou Pavlou 23, Thisio; 🕑 lunch Sun, dinner daily Sep-May, lunch & dinner Jun-Aug; Ⓜ Thisio

It can be hard to get a table on this rooftop terrace with its superb Acropolis views. It's an ideal place for dinner on a summer night, sampling a tasty range of mezedhes, such as grilled cheese, village-style sausage and meatballs.

The stylish bar interiors of Kuzina (p83)

IVIS *Mezedhopoleio* €
☎ 210 323 2554; Navarhou Apostoli 19 (cnr Ivis), Psyrri; M Thisio

This cosy corner eatery, with a few small tables outside, retains a traditional character. It's a good place to enjoy a quiet drink washed down with mezedhes, including excellent prawns and other tasty morsels.

KOUZINA
Modern Greek, Mediterranean €€€
☎ 210 321 5534; Sarri 40, Psyrri; ☽ dinner; M Thisio

Next to the outdoor cinema Cine Psyrri (p87), this former factory has a warm atmosphere, friendly service and a creative menu. There's an impressive glass floor revealing the cellar, and a rooftop terrace with Acropolis views.

KUZINA *Modern Greek* €€
☎ 210 324 0133; Adrianou 9, Psyrri; ☽ lunch & dinner; M Thisio

Kuzina serves creative modern-Greek cuisine in an ambient setting on the pavement next to the Temple of Hephaestus, with the Acropolis looming above. The interior design is superb, as is the view from the rooftop bar.

NIKITAS *Taverna* €
☎ 210 325 2591; Agion Anargyron 19, Psyrri; ☽ noon-6pm; M Monastiraki

Locals swear by this old taverna that has been serving reasonably priced, refreshingly simple and tasty traditional food since well before Psyrri became trendy. It's the only place packed during the day.

OINEAS
Modern/Traditional Greek €€
☎ 210 321 5614; Esopou 9, Psyrri; ☽ 7pm-2.30am Mon, noon-2.30pm Tue-Sun; M Monastiraki

This cheery place on a pedestrian street in Psyrri stands out for the walls of kitsch Greek ads and retro paraphernalia. There are some creative dishes on the menu and excellent generous salads, best shared. Try the cheese pie made with *kataïfi* ('angel hair' pastry).

PIL POUL *Mediterranean, International* €€€
☎ 210 342 3665; Apostolou Pavlou 51 (cnr Poulopoulou), Thisio; ☽ dinner Mon-Sat; M Thisio

For fine dining and romance under the Acropolis, Pil Poul's rooftop terrace is hard to beat. This classy 1920s neoclassical mansion has a modern Mediterranean menu with strong French influences. Dress up and book ahead.

TAVERNA TOU PSYRRI
Taverna €
☎ 210 321 4923; Eshylou 12, Thisio; ☽ 10am-2am; M Monastiraki

One of Psyrri's few remaining authentic tavernas, offering a range of tasty *mayirefta* (ready-cooked meals). It's cheap and cheerful, with quirky murals and interesting old pictures on the walls to amuse you between courses.

TO STEKI TOU ILIA
Taverna €€
☎ 210 345 8052; Eptahalkou 5, Thisio; ☽ lunch & dinner Sun, dinner Tue-Sat; Ⓜ Thisio

Ilia has earned almost celebrity status (and clients) for his lamb chops, sold by the kilo and grilled

to perfection and served with the usual dips, chips and salads. In summer the outdoor tables next to the church are packed.

VAROULKO *Seafood* €€€
☎ 210 522 8400; Pireos 80, Gazi; ☽ dinner Mon-Sat; Ⓜ Keramikos

A winning combination of Acropolis views from the terrace and delicious seafood by celebrated Greek chef Lefteris Lazarou makes this stylish restaurant one of Athens' big culinary treats.

Delighting in the authentic taverna experience at Taverna Tou Psyrri (p83)

WORTH THE TRIP

For great food and a real Athenian neighbourhood ambience, head to the otherwise unremarkable residential area of Ano Petralona. **Therapeftirio** (☎ 210 341 2538; Kallisthenous & Kydantidon 41, Ano Petralona; M Petralona) is one of a cluster of excellent eateries with tables spread on the pavement, its tender calamari grilled to perfection. No frills **Ikonomou** (☎ 210 346 7555; Troon 41 & Kydantidon, Ano Petralona; M Petralona) is renowned for superb, classic home-style dishes, such as *stifadho* (rabbit stew). Nearby, the quirky arthouse cinema **Zefyros** (☎ 210 346 2677; Troon 36, Ano Petralona; M Petralona) screens old classics in a delightful setting. It's a short walk from Petralona metro station.

DRINK

ALEKOS' ISLAND *Bar*
☎ 210 723 9163; Sarri 41, Psyrri; 9.30pm-late; M Thisio
One of Athens' oldest and friendliest gay bars relocated from Kolonaki to this stylish venue. Alekos the artist-owner is behind the bar (some of his works adorn the walls), while partner Jean Pierre plays DJ. Attracts a mixed crowd.

APSENTI *Café-bar*
☎ 210 346 7206; Iraklidon 10, Thisio; 10am-late; M Thisio
Just past the mayhem of the Iraklidon cafés, this casual bar in a neoclassical building is known for its cocktail happy hour, an initiative of friendly Berlin-trained owner Dimitri. It has also introduced food.

CANTINA SOCIAL *Café-bar*
☎ 210 325 1668; Leokoriou 6-8, Psyrri; 10am-late; M Monastiraki

Bars don't come much quirkier than this old haunt down an arcade leading into other buildings and workshops. By day it's full of local workers; at night it cranks up with an alternative crowd.

PEONIA HERBS *Café*
☎ 210 341 0260; Amfiktionos 12, Thisio; 9.30am-8.30pm, closes later on weekends; M Thisio
There's an instantly calming, smoke-free aura to this herb shop and tearoom, where you can sip on a range of exotic teas while it rustles up local herbal remedies in the workshop on the mezzanine.

SOUL *Bar-restaurant*
☎ 210 331 0907; Evripidou 65, Psyrri; 9.30pm-late; M Monastiraki
This impressive, restored neoclassical building has a lively bar, a small club on the 2nd level, an innovative menu and a great garden courtyard for summer. Expect a young

NEIGHBOURHOODS

PSYRRI, THISIO & KERAMIKOS

trendy crowd, good cocktails and a friendly atmosphere.

Y STAVLOS Café-bar
☎ 210 346 7206; Iraklidon 10, Thisio; ⏰ 10am-4am; Ⓜ Thisio
Located in the old royal stables, this is one of the original bars in the thriving Thisio strip. There's a great internal courtyard bar, as well as tables on the pavement outside.

Y THIRIO Bar
☎ 210 722 4104; Lepeniotou 1, Psyrri; Ⓜ Monastiraki

A Psyrri veteran, this Lilliputian bar is a delightful, two-level warren of small nooks and lounges, with eclectic music and unique ambience.

⭐ PLAY

⭐ BIOS Café-bar, Art Space
☎ 210 342 5335; www.bios.gr; Pireos 84, Keramikos; ⏰ 11am-4am; Ⓜ Keramikos
A multifaceted venue popular with an alternative arty crowd and with a lively café and bar. At times you'll find videos screening, per-

Perched atop a roofop garden terrace, the charming outdoor cinema, Cine Psyrri (opposite)

formances on the rooftop, films in the tiny cinema, live bands and exhibitions in various spaces in the rambling former paint factory.

⭐ CINE PSYRRI *Cinema*
☎ 210 324 7234; Sarri 40-44, Psyrri; tickets €7; Ⓜ Thisio

Next to a theatre, this charming outdoor cinema on a rooftop garden terrace is a great place to get some relief from the heat and crowds.

⭐ EL PECADO *Nightclub*
☎ 210 324 4049; Tournavitou 11, Psyrri; admission €10; Ⓨ 9pm-late (closed Jun-Sep); Ⓜ Monastiraki

This winter club has an almost theme-park party feel, where it literally rings the bells to fire up the crowd. It's a sure bet if you want to dance the night away. In summer

it moves beachside to Glyfada (see El Pecado Isla, p146).

⭐ ENVY *Nightclub*
☎ 210 331 7801; Agias Eleousis 3, Psyrri; admission €10; Ⓨ 9pm-late Wed-Sat; Ⓜ Monastiraki

The name of this club seems to change every year, but the massive venue is normally buzzing with a mainstream younger crowd and the latest club and Greek dance music.

⭐ THISSION *Cinema*
☎ 210 342 0864; Apostolou Pavlou 7, Thisio; tickets €7; Ⓜ Thisio

Across from the Acropolis, this is a lovely old-style cinema in a garden setting. Sit towards the back if you want to catch a glimpse of the glowing edifice.

>GAZI & ROUF

Like a beacon, the illuminated red chimneys of the old Athens gasworks lead you to Gazi. Reached on foot from Thisio via pedestrian Ermou, this once semi-industrial area's revival started when the historic gasworks were converted into the Technopolis cultural centre and began hosting concerts and festivals. It wasn't long before restaurants, cool bars and nightclubs sprouted – and spread to neighbouring Rouf. Theatres and cool art spaces in bars and multi-use venues followed. The Benaki Museum's contemporary annexe opened in the grungy thoroughfare of Pireos.

Gazi has also surreptitiously become Athens' gay and lesbian hub, with a gay triangle emerging near the railway line on Leoforos Konstantinoupoleos and Megalou Alexandrou. Nearby Iera Odos is lined with Greek live-music clubs.

GAZI & ROUF

◉ SEE

◉ ATHINAIS

☎ 210 348 0000; www.athinais.com.gr; Kastorias 34-36, Votanikos; exhibitions €3; ⏱ 9.30am-10pm; Ⓜ Keramikos; ♿
This early 20th-century silk factory, converted into a modern arts and cultural complex, hosts temporary art and historical exhibitions and has a cinema, music venue, theatre, café and restaurant.

◉ BENAKI MUSEUM PIREOS ANNEXE

☎ 210 345 3111; www.benaki.gr; Pireos 138 (cnr Andronikou), Rouf; per exhibition €2; ⏱ 10am-6pm Wed, Thu & Sun, 10am-10pm Fri & Sat; Ⓜ Keramikos; ♿
This massive Pireos annexe of the Benaki Museum, housed in a former industrial building, hosts contemporary visual arts, cultural and historical exhibitions, major international shows, and musical performances in the courtyard.

◉ TECHNOPOLIS

☎ 210 346 0981; www.technopolis.gr; Pireos 100; admission free; ⏱ during exhibitions 9am-9pm Mon-Fri; Ⓜ Keramikos; ♿
There's always something on at the city's old gasworks, the impressively restored 1862 complex of furnaces and industrial buildings. It hosts multimedia exhibitions, concerts, festivals and

The futuristic, domed Tholos (p91) theatre is part of the Hellenic Cosmos complex

WORTH THE TRIP

If ruins and museums aren't enough insight into the ancient world, you can take a virtual-reality trip to Ancient Greece via the futuristic Hellenic Cosmos at the **Foundation for the Hellenic World** (off map, A6; ☎ 212 254 0000; www.fhw.gr; Pireos 254, Tavros; adult €5-10, child €4-8 depending on session; ⏱ 9am-9pm Mon-Fri, noon-6pm Sat, 11am-3pm Sun Jun-Sep, check website for winter hr; Ⓜ Kalithea; ♿). The high-tech, domed **Tholos** (admission €10) virtual-reality theatre can take you on an interactive tour of the Ancient Agora, while the Kivotos time-machine has floor-to-ceiling 3D screens featuring ancient Miletus, Olympia and the world of Greek costumes.

special events and has a pleasant café. The small **Maria Callas museum** (⏱ 10am-3pm Mon-Fri) is dedicated to the revered opera diva.

SHOP

SYNAPEIRO *Jewellery*

☎ 210 345 3178; Dekelon 3, Gazi;
Ⓜ Keramikos

The first retail store to open in this otherwise residential/entertainment precinct, this store has contemporary jewellery artfully set against recycled furniture and an old crockery window display.

EAT

🍴 DIRTY GINGER
Modern Greek   €€

☎ 210 342 3809; Triptolemou 46, Gazi;
dinner May-Oct; Ⓜ Keramikos

A summer favourite, with tables around the giant palm tree in the colourfully lit courtyard, this 'post-modern taverna' is big on meat dishes. It's not the place for a quiet

meal as it progressively morphs into a lively bar.

🍴 GAZOHORI
Café, Mezedhopoleio   €

☎ 210 342 4044; Dekeloeon 2, Gazi;
Ⓜ Keramikos

In among Gazi's slick designer eateries, this place stands out for its understated old-style atmosphere and good-value mezedhes. A laid-back younger crowd seems to permanently occupy the pleasant courtyard.

🍴 KANELLA *Traditional Greek* €€

☎ 210 347 6320; Leoforos Konstantinoupoleos 70, Gazi; ⏱ noon-late; Ⓜ Keramikos

Homemade village-style bread, retro mismatched crockery and brown-paper tablecloths set the tone for this trendy taverna opposite the train line. There are daily specials of *mayirefta* (ready-cooked meals) and grills, with a slight modern twist.

🍴 MAMACAS
Traditional Greek €€

☎ 210 346 4984; Persefonis 41, Gazi;
⏱ lunch & dinner Mon-Sat; Ⓜ Keramikos
Decked out in cool white fittings, this Gazi trailblazer kicked off the 'modern taverna' trend, serving home-style food in a chic setting. It has since expanded across the road, added a club and raised prices. It's still popular but has plenty of competition these days.

🍴 SARDELLES
Traditional Greek €€

☎ 210 347 8050; Persefonis 15, Gazi;
⏱ lunch & dinner; Ⓜ Keramikos
This friendly, modern fish taverna, with cutesy fishmonger paper on the tables overlooking the gasworks, specialises in seafood mezedhes. Meat lovers are catered for at the modern grill house next door at Butcher Shop. Both give you a little take-home pot of basil.

🍴 SKOUFIAS *Taverna* €€

☎ 210 341 2252; Vasiliou Tou Megalou 50, Rouf; ⏱ dinner Mon-Sat;
Ⓜ Keramikos
A delightful taverna with tables across the road next to a church, Skoufias dishes up Cretan-style food and an eclectic selection of regional Greek cooking, including game and unusual dishes such as the hearty and tender pork *kotsi* (shank).

🍸 DRINK

🍸 ALIER MAN *Bar-restaurant*

☎ 210 342 6322; Sofroniou 2; Gazi;
Ⓜ Keramikos
A bright and cosy space in two old houses joined around a lovely pebble mosaic courtyard; the charm of this cool bar-restaurant is in the details, such as the painted floral bar, and its easygoing atmosphere.

🍸 BLUE TRAIN *Café-bar*

☎ 210 346 0677; Leoforos Konstanti-noupoleos 84, Gazi; Ⓜ Keramikos
A popular hangout in Gazi's gay triangle, with tables along the rail-way line, this all day bar is a good entrée to gay Athens. The Kazarma club is upstairs and several other gay clubs are clustered nearby.

🍸 GAZAKI *Bar*

☎ 210 346 0901; Triptolemou 31, Gazi;
Ⓜ Keramikos
One of the original Gazi bars still going strong, this friendly and unpretentious place has a lively rooftop terrace and a mixed crowd. The artwork plays on the gasworks theme.

🍸 GAZARTE *Bar*

☎ 210 346 0347; Voutadon 32-34, Gazi;
Ⓜ Keramikos
Upstairs you'll find a cinema-sized screen playing cartoons and videos,

great city views, mainstream music and a trendy 30-something crowd.

HOXTON *Bar*

☎ 210 341 3395; Voutadon 42, Gazi; Ⓜ Keramikos

Since the metro station opened, the drinkers along the Voutadon strip of bars flow into one big throng. Hoxton is one of the most popular bars, with funky industrial design, clashing leather chesterfields and modern art.

PLAY

K44 *Bar, Art Space*

☎ 210 342 6804; Leoforos Konstantinoupoleos 33, Gazi; ✆ closed Aug; Ⓜ Keramikos

This two-level multi-use warehouse on the railway line is the 'in' place for the hip and alternative arts scene. The front bar is a vast concrete space hosting alternative DJ nights and special events, with art exhibitions and artists studios upstairs.

NIPIAGOGIO *Bar-club*

☎ 210 345 8534; cnr Kleanthou & Elasidou, Gazi; Ⓜ Keramikos

One of the first bars to open in Gazi, this popular place in a former kindergarten (as the name in Greek suggests) plays on the

CLUBBING GREEK STYLE

Gazi is one of the hubs of Athens Greek nightclub scene, with live shows at cabaret-style entertainment venues along Iera Odos and Pireos (D4), where hedonism reigns. You can catch anything from top performers to the extravagant *bouzoukia*, where free-spending flower-throwing men admire the scantily clad women dancing sensually to the sound of crooning singers. Some of the biggest and best shows in town can be seen at the massive high-tech **Athinon Arena** (☎ 210 347 111; Pireos 166, Gazi; Ⓜ Keramikos), while leading acts can be seen at **Iera Odos** (☎ 210 342 8272; 18-20 Iera Odos, Gazi; Ⓜ Keramikos). During summer the action heads to the big beach clubs (see Summer Clubbing, p146).

children's toy theme in its décor. Inside it's one of the liveliest small clubs, while there's a fantastic courtyard for summer.

SODADE *Nightclub*

☎ 210 346 8657; www.sodade.gr; Triptolemou 10, Gazi; admission €7.50; ✆ 11pm-late; Ⓜ Keramikos

Two clubs in one, with mainstream dance music in the front bar and more progressive rhythms out the back. Sodade gets very busy come evening and attracts a stylish, young, gay-friendly crowd.

>OMONIA & METAXOURGHIO

Bustling Plateia Omonias (Omonia Sq) isn't the best introduction to Athens, but it is a colourful, if gritty, part of the city's commercial district. Once one of Athens' grand squares, the traffic-clogged roundabout has undergone several unpopular facelifts. Despite clean-up efforts, and the arrival of a few hip hotel and bars, the areas around Omonia retain a seedy character, attracting less desirable elements at night.

Omonia is a key axis in the commercial triangle of Athens' historic centre – bordered by Stadiou, Athinas and Ermou in the south – a grid of narrow streets with shops selling almost anything, often neatly clustered thematically (eg ties or door handles). Pedestrian Eolou takes you past pretty Plateia Kotzia and the town hall, while Athinas leads to the bazaar-like central market. West of the market is the unofficial Asian quarter, where many of the city's new arrivals congregate.

Neighbouring Metaxourghio is the next candidate for urban renewal. New galleries have opened and it's an emerging hotspot for restaurants and bars.

OMONIA & METAXOURGHIO

🔘 SEE
Athens Municipal Art
Gallery **1** B3
Breeder.......................**2** A1
Gazon Rouge **3** C1
Hellenic Cultural
Centre......................**4** D1
Hondos Center.............**5** D1
Olympic Airways **6** D1
Rebecca Camhi
Gallery **7** B2

🛍 SHOP
Athens Central Market ...**8** D4
Lesvos Shop.................**9** D4
Meat Market...............**10** D4
Notos Galleries **11** E2
Skedio & Kosmima **12** F3
To Pantopoleion...........**13** E3
Xylouris.......................**14** F3

🍴 EAT
Aigaion **15** F2
Archeon Gefsis **16** A1

Athinaikon...................**17** E2
Diporto Agoras............**18** C3
Hell's Kitchen **19** D3
Kriti............................**20** E1
Sappho **21** A2
Taverna Papandreou **22** D4
Telis **23** C4

⭐ PLAY
Bar Guru Bar...............**24** C3
National Theatre of
Greece.....................**25** C1
Stoa Athanaton **26** D3

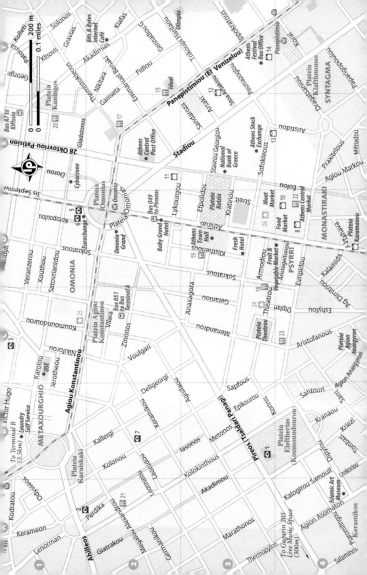

SEE

ATHENS MUNICIPAL ART GALLERY

☎ 210 324 3023; Pireos 51, Plateia Eleftherias (Koumoundourou), Omonia; admission free; ⏲ 9am-1pm & 5-9pm Mon-Fri, 9am-1pm Sun; Ⓜ Thisio

The municipality's rich collection includes more than 2300 works from leading 19th- and 20th-century Greek artists, including works from the acclaimed '30s generation, as well as a fine collection of engravings.

SHOP

ATHENS CENTRAL MARKET
Market

Athinas (btwn Sofokleous & Evripidou), Omonia; ⏲ 7am-3pm Mon-Sat; Ⓜ Omonia

The hectic, colourful Athens *agora* (market; also referred to as the Varvakios Agora) is the highlight of the vibrant Athinas market district. It's a sensory and gastronomic delight, with an amazing range of olives, spices, cheeses and deli treats. The historic meat market, with hanging carcasses illuminated by swinging

Grabbing a selection of dried goods at the Athens Central Market

ART MOVEMENTS

It's no surprise that arts trailblazer **Rebecca Camhi** (☎ 210 523 3049; www.rebeccacamhi .com; Leonidou 9, Metaxourghio; ☾ noon-8pm Tue-Fri, noon-5pm Sat; Ⓜ Metaxourghio) opened her new gallery in the up-and-coming arts precinct of Metaxourghio. She was among the first to bring art downtown near Psyrri; and the hip galleries are on the move again. Experimental gallery **Breeder** (☎ 210 331 7527; www.thebreedersystem.com; Iasonos 45, Metaxourghio; Ⓜ Metaxourghio) relocated from Psyrri, while **Gazon Rouge** (☎ 210 524 8077; www.gazonrouge.com; Victor Hugo 15, Metaxourghio; ☾ noon-8pm Tue-Fri, noon-4pm Sat; Ⓜ Metaxourghio) was the first to move into the 'hood, setting up a gallery and art publishing house with a bookstore and café.

light bulbs, is a surreal highlight. The tavernas in and around the market are worth seeking out (p99).

🛍 LESVOS SHOP Food & Drink
☎ 210 321 7395; Athinas 33, Omonia; Ⓜ Monastiraki
As well as a large selection of ouzo (29 kinds at last count), this store (off map, D1) sells traditional products made by local women's cooperatives on the islands of Lesvos and Limnos, including biscuits and sweet fruit preserves. There's also a great range of cheese, honey and other goodies.

🛍 NOTOS GALLERIES
Department Store
☎ 210 324 5811; Eolou 2-8, Omonia; Ⓜ Omonia
One of Athens' oldest department stores, Notos has a respectable range of Greek and imported labels in clothing, footwear, cosmetics and personal goods, and a dedi-

cated homewares store on Plateia Kotzia (E3).

🛍 SKEDIO & KOSMIMA
Jewellery
☎ 210 331 2077; Stoa Arsakiou (off Panepistimiou), Omonia; Ⓜ Panepistimio
Blink and you might miss this tiny treasure trove in a grand old arcade. You can barely do a 360-degree turn, but the shop is crammed with lovely contemporary pieces by local jewellers.

🛍 TO PANTOPOLEION
Food & Wine
☎ 210 323 4612; Sofokleous 1 (cnr Aristidou), Omonia; Ⓜ Panepistimio
From Santorini capers to boutique olive oils and rusks from Crete, this excellent store has traditional food products from around Greece. There are jars of sweets, a large selection of Greek wines and spirits, and a fresh deli if you can't wait until you get home.

NEIGHBOURHOODS

OMONIA & METAXOURGHIO

XYLOURIS *Music*
☎ 210 322 2711; www.xylouris.gr;
Panepistimiou 39 (in arcade), Omonia;
Ⓜ **Panepistimio**
This small music trove, run by the
family of the late Cretan legend
Nikos Xylouris, has a comprehensive range of traditional Greek
music and a good world-music
section.

🍴 EAT

🍴 AIGAION *Sweets* €
☎ 210 381 4621; Panepistimiou 46,
Omonia; 🕐 8am-11pm, closed Sun;
Ⓜ **Omonia**
Since 1826, this no-frills basement haunt has served up an
endless supply of *loukoumadhes*
(ball-shaped doughnuts) served
with honey and walnuts. There are
also cheese pies and other sweets,
such as rice pudding.

🍴 ARCHEON GEFSIS
Traditional Greek €€
☎ 210 523 9661; Kodratou 22, Metax-
ourghio; 🕐 lunch & dinner Mon-Sat;
Ⓜ **Metaxourghio**
This themed restaurant has
surprisingly good food based on
ancient Greek cuisine, including
delicious roast meats served with
purées of peas, chickpeas and vegetables. Waiters wear flowing red
robes, while diners sip wine from
earthenware cups and use spoons

instead of forks, as the ancients
did. Bookings essential.

🍴 ATHINAIKON
Mezedhopoleio €€
☎ 210 383 8485; Themistokleous 2 (cnr
Panepistimiou), Omonia; 🕐 lunch & dinner Mon-Sat, closed Aug; Ⓜ **Omonia**
This friendly Athens institution
has a wide selection of reliable
traditional mezedhes and seafood
dishes and an old-world atmosphere (it's been around since
1932).

Dishing up traditional mezedhes, Athinaikon

NEIGHBOURHOODS

OMONIA & METAXOURGHIO

🍴 DIPORTO AGORAS
Taverna   €

☎ 210 321 1463; Theatrou 1 (cnr Sokratous), Omonia; 🕐 8am-6pm Mon-Sat, closed mid-Aug; Ⓜ Omonia

Near the Athens Central Market, there's no signage, only two doors leading to a rustic cellar taverna where the handful of dishes hasn't changed in years. The staples are delicious chickpea soup, grilled fish, fried potatoes and salad, washed down with mandatory wine (they don't ask) from the barrels lining the wall. The often-erratic service is part of the appeal.

🍴 HELL'S KITCHEN
Café-bar, Restaurant   €€

☎ 210 524 1555; Klisthenous 13, Omonia; Ⓜ Omonia

Behind the town hall, this newcomer is a great place to lunch on wholesome burgers and western-style cuisine. In the evenings it livens up with drinkers sipping mojitos, watching the area's seedier elements parade by.

🍴 KRITI *Taverna*   €

☎ 210 382 6998; Veranzerou 5, Plateia Kaningos, Omonia; Ⓜ Omonia

Down an innocuous old arcade, this tiny place is popular with nostalgic Cretans, students and those wanting some good-value traditional Cretan food, old-world ambience and fiery *raki* (Cretan fire water).

TO MARKET, TO MARKET

After a big night out, Athenians venture into the darkened central meat market of the Athens Central Market in search of a steaming bowl of hangover-busting *patsa* (tripe soup) at **Taverna Papandreou** (☎ 210 321 4970; Aristogeitonos 1, Omonia; Ⓜ Omonia), tucked at the back of the meat section. If that doesn't take your fancy, you can choose from the huge pots and trays of tasty, traditional dishes, 24 hours a day (closed Sunday night). The tavern has lost some of its quaint rustic charm in its recent makeover, but there's still something truly memorable, however, about exiting at dawn as the market traders start hanging the meat out.

🍴 SAPPHO *Mezedhopoleio*   €

☎ 210 523 6447; Meg Alexandrou 35, Metaxourghio; 🕐 lunch & dinner, closed Aug; Ⓜ Metaxourghio

Fine regional specialities from Lesvos are not the only traditions from the island at play here. The understated lesbian theme carries through to the décor and the owners run a popular summer cantina on the island (which inspired the very term).

🍴 TELIS *Taverna*   €

☎ 210 324 2775; Evripidou 86, Omonia; 🕐 breakfast, lunch & dinner, closed mid-Aug; Ⓜ Monastiraki

It doesn't get more basic than this fluoro-lit, bare-walled,

NEIGHBOURHOODS

OMONIA & METAXOURGHIO

paper-tableclothed Athens institution. Since the '70s, Telis has been slaving over the flame-grill cooking his famous pork chops to perfection. They go down nicely with the house wine or beer.

⭐ PLAY

⭐ BAR GURU BAR
Bar-restaurant

☎ 210 324 6530; www.bargurubar.gr; Plateia Theatrou 10, Omonia; 🕒 9pm-late; Ⓜ Omonia

The popular Bar Guru Bar has Thai food coming out of the kitchen downstairs and live jazz upstairs, in this intimate space in the grungy square behind the markets.

⭐ GREEK NATIONAL OPERA
Theatre

☎ 210 361 2461; www.nationalopera.gr; Olympia Theatre; Akadimias 59, Omonia; Ⓜ Omonia

The Greek National Opera (Ethniki Lyriki Skini) season runs from November to June. Performances are usually held at the Olympia theatre or at the Odeon of Herodes Atticus in summer.

⭐ NATIONAL THEATRE OF GREECE *Theatre*

☎ 210 522 0585; www.n-t.gr; Agiou Konstantinou 22, Omonia; Ⓜ Omonia

Designed by Ernst Ziller, the columned façade of this 1901

The decoratively styled façade of the National Theatre of Greece

WORTH THE TRIP
One of the most dynamic rock-music venues in town is **Gagarin 205 Live Music Space** (off map, A4; ☎ 210 854 7601; www.gagarin205.gr; Liossion 205, Thimarakia; Ⓜ Keramikos; ⏱ from 9.30pm). The 1200-seat venue hosts top international touring acts, as well as local indie bands of various musical persuasions. It occasionally runs cult film festivals and other events.

building was inspired in part by Hadrian's Library; the interior was based on Vienna's People's Theatre. It served as the Royal Theatre for the king's guests until 1908.

Damaged in the 1999 earthquake, it underwent a major refurbishment and was due to raise the curtain in 2008.

⭐ STOA ATHANATON
Rembetika Club
☎ 210 321 4362; Sofokleous 19, Athens Central Market, Omonia; ⏱ 3-7.30pm & 11pm-late Mon-Sat; Ⓜ Omonia
Located in the middle of Athens Central Market, this classic *rembetika* (Greek blues) club has been around since 1930. It is open day and night and is always lively, with veteran *rembetes* (exponents of *rembetika*) and loyal patrons.

>EXARHIA

Near the National Archaeological Museum, laid-back, bohemian Exarhia has an alternative culture and history that sets it apart from Athens' newly hip districts. Although partly gentrified, particularly towards Strefi Hill, the neighbourhood retains a youthful and unconventional identity, thanks to a resident population of students (it's near the universities), artists, actors, old lefties and intellectuals. Exarhia's anarchic reputation is a throwback to its associations with radical politics and the infamous student sit-in at the Athens Polytechnio (Technical University), under the junta. Despite the omnipresent graffiti, riot police on the periphery and the odd tame incident evoking its revolutionary days, it's a safe and relaxed neighbourhood.

Exarhia has an eclectic mix of comic stores, record shops, publishing houses, computer and alternative book and clothing stores. It has a vibrant bar scene, particularly the crowded cheap student hangouts on Mesolongiou, good-value eateries and rock and *rembetika* (Greek blues) clubs. Plateia Exarhion (Exarhion Sq) is the neighbourhood's focal point, with many tavernas along pedestrian Valtestiou and Benaki, and bustling cafés and bars around nearly every corner.

EXARHIA

SEE

EPIGRAPHICAL MUSEUM

☎ 210 821 7637; www.culture.gr;
Tositsa 1; admission free; ☼ 8.30am-
3pm Tue-Sun; Ⓜ Viktoria; ☐

This 'library of stones' houses an
important collection of Greek in-
scriptions detailing official records,
including lists of war dead, tribute
lists showing annual payments
by Athens' allies, and the decree
ordering the evacuation of Athens
before the 480 BC Persian invasion.

NATIONAL ARCHAEOLOGICAL MUSEUM

☎ 210 821 7717; www.culture.gr; 28
Oktovriou-Patission 44; adult/child €7/3;
☼ 8am-7pm Tue-Sun Apr-Oct, 10am-
3pm Mon, 8am-3pm Tue-Sun Nov-Mar;
Ⓜ Viktoria, ☐ 2, 4, 5, 9, 11; ☐

Allow plenty of time to view the
vast and spectacular collection of
Greece's pre-eminent museum
(see p14 for more details), with
prized finds from Greece's archaeological sites.

SHOP

THYMARI TOU STREFI
Food & Wine

☎ 210 330 0384; Kalidromiou
51A; Ⓜ Omonia

Right in the thick of Saturday's
lively street market (right), this
quaint deli has a delectable array

SATURDAY BAZAAR

Every Saturday morning locals make the
trek up to the Kalidromiou (D3), in the
foothills of Strefi Hill, to Exarhia's weekly
farmers market (☼ 6am-2pm; Kalidromiou; ☐ 026 or Ⓜ Omonia) or laïki
agora, an enduring Athens institution.
This is one of the city's most atmospheric
markets, with rowdy traders taking over
one of Exarhia's finest streets, lined with
lovely neoclassical buildings and set
against the dramatic backdrop of Lykavittos Hill in the distance. It's mostly fresh
produce and household goods, but it's a
real Athenian neighbourhood experience.
Get a prime seat at one of the busy cafés.

of traditional products, honey,
cheese and regional specialities, as
well as organic wine and ouzo.

TUBE Fashion

☎ 210 382 7706; Solonos 114; Ⓜ Omonia

This store has an interesting range
of edgy youthful women's fashion
at this emerging alternative (and
affordable) clothing precinct on
busy Solonos, heading west from
Kolonaki.

VINYL MICROSTORE Music

☎ 210 361 4544; www.vmradio.gr;
Didotou 34; Ⓜ Panepistimio

A drop-in centre for serious music
fans who can sample the eclectic
indie, alternative and dance vinyl
releases and CDs over a coffee. An
online radio station broadcasts

live from the mezzanine. The owners organise party tours, art exhibitions in the basement and an indie music festival.

EAT

BARBAGIANNIS *Taverna* €
☎ 210 330 0185; Emmanuel Benaki 94; ⏱ lunch & dinner; Ⓜ Omonia

An Exarhia institution, this low-key *mayirio* (cook house) is popular with students and those wanting good-value home-style Greek food. Choose from the variety of big trays of traditional dishes, such as *pastitsio* (layers of baked macaroni and minced meat), washed down with house wine.

BYZANTINO TOU STREFI *Mezedhopoleio* €
☎ 6947378285; Strefi Hill (enter from steps near Emmanuel Benaki 126); ⏱ 6pm-late Mon-Fri; 10am-late Sat & Sun; Ⓜ Omonia

Escape up to Strefi Hill to this casual mezedhopoleio, where you can enjoy good-value mezedhes in a peaceful setting away from the urban jungle.

FOOD COMPANY *International* €
☎ 210 380 5004; Emmanuel Benaki 63-65; ☎ 10am-2am; Ⓜ Omonia

This Kolonaki favourite has found a cheery new home in Exarhia. The casual café-style eatery serves a range of healthy salads, wholesome hot and cold pasta and noodle dishes. The cheesecake is delicious.

ROZALIA *Taverna* €
☎ 210 330 2933; Valtetsiou 58; ⏱ lunch & dinner; Ⓜ Omonia

A veteran family-run taverna, this place is popular for the huge

Chilling out at the shady courtyard garden, Rozalia

Nektarios Pappas
Founder, Vinyl Microstore (p104) & VM Internet Radio

Exarhia in one word Restless. **In 25 words or less** It's changing face with more mainstream shops opening. It's still politically active. There's a lot of creativity and alternative stores. It's definitely not trendy. **Anarchy in Exarhia?** It's an accepted part of the neighbourhood; it's not dangerous. It's healthy to have a neighbourhood like Exarhia, it's like the city's pressure valve, where people let off steam. You get a sense of what's happening from the posters and the graffiti. **Best local cheap taverna** Barbagiannis (p105), or I take visiting bands to Kriti (p99), at Plateai Kaningos. **Favourite bars** Kazu (p108), a small bar with great cocktails and good music. Alexandrino (opposite) for a quiet drink or Booze Cooperativa (p47) in the centre. Petit Fleur (p120) in Kolonaki is stylish and plays old jazz records. **Interesting alternative Greek music** Guitarist Babis Papadopoulos; '80s new-wave influenced Victory Collapse; Drogertek for experimental jazz.

courtyard garden with fans spraying water to keep you cool. Excellent-value grilled meats, traditional cooking and decent house wine ensure it's always lively.

SKOUFIAS *Mezedhopoleio* €

☎ 210 382 8206; Lontou 4; Ⓜ Omonia

This little place has a more urban vibe than its sister restaurant in Gazi (p92), but nonetheless is a great choice for regional Greek cuisine with a distinct Cretan influence. Try the rabbit stew or Cretan salad.

YIANTES *Modern Greek* €€

☎ 210 330 1369; Valtetsiou 44; Ⓜ Omonia

This is a smart, modern taverna set in a lovely garden courtyard next to the open-air cinema. Yiantes has excellent regional cuisine and creative dishes made with organic produce.

Y DRINK

Y ALEXANDRINO *Bar*

☎ 210 382 7780; Emmanuel Benaki 69a; Ⓜ Omonia

There's a quaint French bistro feel to this tiny bar on the e1merging

Earthy red chic to go with its organic cuisine, Yiantes

dining and bar strip along Benaki. Alexandrino is great for a quiet drink; the service is friendly and you can sit at the narrow bar or at the few tables on the pavement.

▼ CIRCUS *Bar*
☎ 210 361 5255; Navarinou 11; Ⓜ Panepistimio

Right on the border of Kolonaki and Exarhia, Circus has Exarhia's youthful edge without the grunge and a bit of Kolonaki's glamour without the pretensions. Most nights there's a fun vibe and great music.

▼ KAZU *Bar*
☎ 210 360 2242; Mavromihali 3; Ⓜ Panepistimio

A bright and cheery little bar with a penchant for black, soulful sounds, good cocktails and a hip 30-something crowd.

▼ TRALALA *Café*
☎ 210 362 8066; Asklipiou 45; Ⓜ Panepistimio

This arty hangout on the outskirts of Exarhia, popular with actors, does a roaring coffee trade by day, while in the evening the cool crowd spills out onto the pavement.

▼ WUNDERBAR *Bar*
☎ 210 381 8577; Themistokleous 80; ⏱ 10am-late; Ⓜ Omonia

A trendy lounge bar and café on Plateia Exarhion (Exarhion Sq),

this is a good place to start the evening before exploring the side streets.

★ PLAY

★ AN CLUB *Live Music*
☎ 210 330 5056; Solomou 13-15; ⏱ 9.30pm-late; Ⓜ Omonia

Exarhia's popular basement rock club hosts lesser-known international bands, as well as some interesting local acts.

★ DECADENCE *Live Music*
☎ 210 882 3544; Vasiliou Voulgaroktonou 69 (cnr Poulherias), Strefi Hill; Ⓜ Omonia

Popular with students and a younger crowd, you'll hear the gamut of cool music at this rock bar, which holds weekly events. It's housed in a neoclassical building near Strefi Hill.

★ KAVOURAS *Rembetika*
☎ 210 381 0202; Themistokleous 64; admission €6; ⏱ 11pm-late, closed Aug; Ⓜ Omonia

Above Exarhia's all-night souvlaki joint, this lively club has a decent line-up of musicians playing *rembetika* until dawn. No cover charge after 1am.

★ REBETIKI ISTORIA *Rembetika*
off map, D5; ☎ 210 642 4937; Ippokratous 181; ⏱ 11pm-late; Ⓜ Panepistimio

One of the older *rembetika* haunts, with an authentic smoky atmosphere, dedicated regulars and a wall of old photos of *rembetika* musicians. It's casual, relaxed and affordable, and thus popular with students.

⭐ RIVIERA *Cinema*

☎ 210 383 7716; Valtetsiou 46; tickets €7; Ⓜ Omonia

Catch the latest flick at this charming outdoor cinema in a lovely garden courtyard setting on a pedestrian street.

⭐ TAXIMI *Rembetika*

off map, D4; ☎ 210 363 9919; Isavron 29 (cnr Harilaou Trikoupi); ⏰ 11pm-late Tue-Sat; Ⓜ Panepistimio

Most of Greece's major *rembetika* exponents have played here since it opened 20 years ago at the beginning of the *rembetika* revival. It has gone a little upmarket – and expensive – but it is still a popular for authentic *rembetika*. It's best to go weeknights as it gets packed.

>KOLONAKI

Kolonaki is an adjective as much as a suburb: it's the neighbourhood that most epitomises the Athenian elite's ambitions and pretensions. Undeniably chic, Kolonaki is where old money mixes with the nouveau-riche and wannabes. On Plateia Kolonakiou (Kolonaki Sq) you'll find the original people-watching cafés teeming with yuppies, actors, politicians, journalists and a passing parade of aristocratic old Athenian ladies, style queens and glitzy fashion victims. The cool younger set frequents the bars on Skoufa, Haritos and Ploutarhou.

Named after a tiny obscure column in the square, Kolonaki stretches from Syntagma to the foothills of Lykavittos Hill, and is home to the prime minister's residence, embassies, excellent private museums and stylish apartment blocks.

Heading up from the main square, the streets are full of chic boutiques, upmarket restaurants and galleries. Things get more sedate and

KOLONAKI

SEE
Benaki Museum 1 D6
Byzantine & Christian
   Museum 2 F6
Chapel of Agios
   Georgios 3 E2
Goulandris Museum of
   Cycladic & Ancient
   Greek Art 4 D6
Lykavittos Hill 5 G1
Museum of the History
   of Greek Costume 6 B4
War Museum 7 F6

SHOP
Apivita 8 C4
Apriati 9 C4
Astrolavos Art Life 10 E6
Bettina 11 D4
Danos 12 D5

Elena Votsi 13 D5
Fanourakis 14 E5
Goutis 15 C4
Kalogirou 16 D5
Koukoutsi 17 B2
Lak 18 C5
Luisa 19 C5
Me Me Me 20 D5
Petai Petai 21 C4
Prasini 22 D5
Ropa Lavada 23 B4
Vassilis Zoulias Old
   Athens 24 C5
Vraki 25 B3

EAT
Amada 26 B5
Fasoli 27 A2
Filippou 28 E4
Oikeio 29 F5
Orizontes 30 E3

Ouzadiko 31 F5
Papadakis 32 C4
Ta Kioupia 33 G3

DRINK
City 34 F4
Frame 35 D4
Mai Tai 36 F5
Mommy 37 B2
Petit Fleur 38 B4
Rock'N'Roll 39 E6
Rosebud 40 B3
Skoufaki 41 B4

PLAY
Baraki Tou Vasili 42 B3
Dexameni 43 D4

Please see over for map

residential in the streets towards Lykavittos. Unlike other hip and trendy neighbourhoods, Kolonaki is what it's always been – solid, good fun and ever-fashionable.

SEE

◉ BENAKI MUSEUM
☎ 210 367 1000; www.benaki.gr; Koumbari 1 (cnr Vasilissis Sofias); admission €6, ⏱ 9am-5pm Mon, Wed, Fri & Sat, 9am-midnight Thu, 9am-3pm Sun; Ⓜ Syntagma; ♿

The Benaki (see p20) is the must-see of Athens' private museums, with a superb collection and a great café-restaurant on the terrace.

◉ BYZANTINE & CHRISTIAN MUSEUM
☎ 210 721 1027; www.culture.gr; Leoforos Vasilissis Sofias 22; adult/conc

€4/2; ⏱ 8.30am-7pm Tue-Sun May-Sep, 8.30am-3pm Oct-Apr; Ⓜ Syntagma; ♿

A priceless collection of Christian art that sheds light on the Byzantine and post-Byzantine worlds set in a lovely museum in the stunning grounds of an historic Athenian estate (p24).

◉ LYKAVITTOS HILL
☎ 210 722 7092; funicular return €5; ⏱ funicular 9am-11.45pm, every 30min; Ⓜ Evangelismos

A funicular rail car (which leaves from the corner of Aristippou and Ploutarhou) takes you up to cool breezes and superb views on the

The whitewashed Chapel of Agios Georgios is perched on the rocky outcrop of Lykavittos Hill

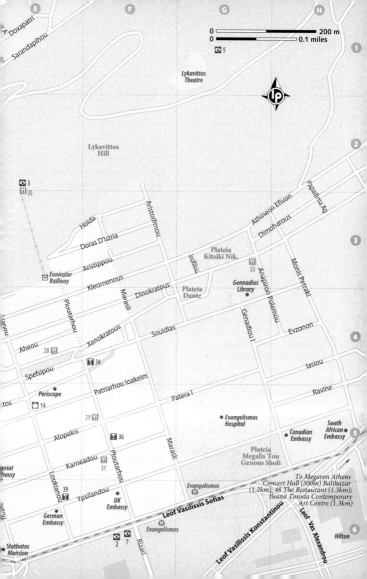

E Doxapatri
A. Doxapatri
E. Sarandapihou

F

G

H

0 ──────── 200 m
0 ──────── 0.1 miles

🕐 5

Lykavittos
Theatre

1

Lykavittos
Hill

2

🕐 3
🍴 30

Hoida

Doras D'Istria

Aristippou

Aristodimou

Iofidou

Athineon Efivon

Papadima Ag

Dimoharous

3

Plateia
Kitsiki Nik.

🍴 33

🚠 Funicular
Railway

Kleomenous

Dinokratous

Plateia
Dante

Gennadius
Library

Anapiron Polemou

Monis Petraki

Marasli

Genadiou I.

Evzonon

4

Aheou

28 🍴

Xenokratous

Souidias

Iasiou

Spefsipou

34 🍴

Patriarhou Ioakeim

Patera I

Ravine

Periscope

📷 14

29 🍴

Evangelismos
Hospital

Canadian
Embassy

South
African
Embassy

5

Alopekis

36 🍴

Karneadou

31 🍴

Plateia
Megalis Tou
Genous Sholi

To Megaron Athens
Concert Hall (500m) Balthazar
(1.2km); 48 The Restaurant (1.3km);
Ileana Tounta Contemporary
Art Centre (1.3km)

Ploutarhou

39 🍴

Ypsilandou

UK
Embassy

Ⓜ Evangelismos

Marasli

Loukianou

...riot
...bassy

German
Embassy

Ⓜ Evangelismos

Leof Vasilissis Sofias

Rizari

🕐 2 🕐 7

Leof Vasilissis Konstantinou

Leof Vas. Alexandrou

Stathatos
Mansion

Hilton

6

Ploutarhou

Spefsipou

Marasli

...tos

NEIGHBOURHOODS

KOLONAKI

summit of Lykavittos (see also Athens from Above, p19). Summer concerts are held at the open-air theatre on the northern side; see Athens Festival, p27 for more details. There are two cannons just below on the western side of the hill that fire salutes on special occasions. Regular church services are held at the Chapel of Agios Georgios, the most important being on 23 April, the day of the patron saint, St George, and Good Friday, when there is a moving candlelight procession along the hill.

☑ GOULANDRIS MUSEUM OF CYCLADIC & ANCIENT GREEK ART

☎ 210 722 8321; www.cycladic.gr; **Neofytou Douka 4 (cnr Leoforos Vasilissis Sofias); admission €5;** ⏰ **10am-4pm Mon, Wed-Fri (to 8pm Wed Jun-Aug), 10am-3pm Sat;** Ⓜ **Evangelismos;** ♿
This exceptional private museum boasts the biggest independent collection of distinctive Cycladic art and holds excellent periodic exhibitions. See p23 for further information.

☑ MUSEUM OF THE HISTORY OF GREEK COSTUME

☎ **210 362 9513; Dimokritou 7; admission free;** ⏰ **10am-2pm Mon-Fri, 5-10pm Thu, closed Aug;** Ⓜ **Syntagma**
Run by the Lyceum of Greek Women, this museum has changing exhibi-

tions from its comprehensive collection of regional costumes, jewellery and accessories. The gift shop sells books on folk culture and handmade crafts.

☑ WAR MUSEUM

☎ **210 724 4464; Rizari 2 (cnr Leoforos Vasilissis Sofias); admission free;** ⏰ **9am-2pm Tue-Sun;** Ⓜ **Evangelismos;** ♿
Kids love climbing into the fighter planes in the forecourt of this junta-era museum honouring Greece's armed forces. It has an invaluable historical collection of war memorabilia, including weapons, maps, armour and models of battles.

Goulandris Museum of Cycladic & Ancient Greek Art

CLASSICAL MUSIC

Athens' classical-music scene centres on the state-of-the-art **Megaron Athens Concert Hall** (off map, H5; ☎ 210 728 2333-7; www.megaron.gr; Leoforos Vasilissis Sofias, Ambelokipi; M Megaro Moussikis) from October to June. The multifunction-venue has superb acoustics, excellent facilities, as well as an exhibition hall that serves as a temporary home for the National Museum of Contemporary Art (under construction).

 # SHOP

◻ APIVITA *Beauty*
☎ 210 364 0760; www.apivita.com; Solonos 26; M Syntagma
Apivita's flagship store has the full range of its excellent natural beauty products and an express spa downstairs for pampering on the run.

◻ APRIATI *Jewellery*
☎ 210 360 7878; www.apriati.com; Pindarou 29; M Syntagma
Apriati has a tempting original range of contemporary jewellery designed by young duo Athena Axioti and Themis Bobolas. There's another branch in Syntagma (p44).

◻ ASTROLAVOS ART LIFE
Art Gallery
☎ 210 722 1200; www.astrolavos.gr; Irodotou 11; M Evangelismos

This trendy art store has small sculptures and works by local artists, while the gallery downstairs sells bigger works by well-known contemporary Greek and Greek-American artists. There is an exhibition space on the ground level.

◻ BETTINA *Fashion*
☎ 210 323 8759; Pindarou 40 (cnr Anagnostopoulou); M Syntagma
This chic boutique has three levels of top-name fashion, including creations by Greek fashion queen Sophia Kokosalaki, Angelos Frentzos and other well-known local and international designers.

◻ DANOS *Shoes*
☎ 210 362 5390; Plateia Filikis Eterias 6; M Evangelismos
Artful window displays showcase Danos' feminine, individual designs, made in Greece from the finest imported leathers. There is also a select range of international designs.

◻ ELENA VOTSI *Jewellery*
☎ 210 360 0936; www.elenavotsi.com; Xanthou 7; M Evangelismos
Votsi is renowned for her original, big and bold designs using exquisite semiprecious stones, which sell in New York and London. Her profile was boosted when she was chosen to design the new Olympic Games medal.

▢ FANOURAKIS *Jewellery*
☎ 210 721 1762; Patriarhou Ioakeim 23;
Ⓜ Syntagma

Delicate pieces of folded gold characterise Fanourakis' bows, insects and other unique creations. The distinctive designs are sheer art, a factor that is also reflected in the prices.

▢ GOUTIS *Antiques*
☎ 210 361 3557; Dimokritou 10;
Ⓜ Syntagma

Packed into this tiny treasure trove of a store you'll find an eclectic collection of antiques and collectables, mostly from Greece and France, including jewellery worn with traditional dress, prints, silverware, royal crockery and embroideries.

▢ KALOGIROU *Shoes*
☎ 210 722 8804; Patriarhou Ioakeim 4;
Ⓜ Evangelismos

Shoe fetishists will love the offerings in colours and styles to blow the imagination and budget, with top international designers and Kologirou's own creations. Avoid the Saturday morning rush by the boutique set.

▢ KOUKOUTSI *Fashion*
☎ 210 361 4060; Skoufa 81;
Ⓜ Syntagma

A tiny store with a novel range of graphic T-shirts and accessories, including its original designs featuring Athens architectural landmarks and funky T-shirts by international designers.

▢ LAK *Fashion*
☎ 210 628 3260; Skoufa 10;
Ⓜ Syntagma

Lak offers Greek designer Lakis Gavalas' brand of women's and men's daywear and accessories with a hip edge.

▢ LUISA *Fashion*
☎ 210 363 5600; Skoufa 17; Ⓜ Syntagma

Fashionistas and dreamers will love the A-list international designers at this super-chic emporium, including Roberto Cavalli, Gaultier, Missoni and Chloé.

▢ ME ME ME
Fashion & Accessories
☎ 210 722 4890; Haritos 19;
Ⓜ Evangelismos

This colourful boutique has a range of youthful clothing, bijoux and accessories from local designer brands, including Meatpacking District, Bed of Roses, Fairy Tales, Two in A Gondola and Pavlos Kyriakidis.

▢ PETAI PETAI *Jewellery*
☎ 210 362 4315; Skoufa 30;
Ⓜ Syntagma

This narrow store has cabinets full of eclectic designs from leading local designers, from casual silver pieces to handcrafted gold with precious stones.

PRASINI *Shoes*
☎ 210 364 1590; Tsakalof 7-9;
Ⓜ Evangelismos

A two-level shoe heaven, with French, Italian, Spanish and Greek designer footwear for the really well-heeled. You may find a bargain in the basement.

ROPA LAVADA
Women's Fashion
☎ 210 361 6591; Solonos 42;
Ⓜ Syntagma

The quirky window display is reason enough to check out this store on the alternative clothing strip of Solonos, halfway to Exarhia. There's a range of youthful casual wear from Greek and foreign designers.

The eye-catching window-display items of Ropa Lavada

VASSILIS ZOULIAS OLD ATHENS *Shoes*
☎ **210 361 4762; Kanari 17;**
Ⓜ **Syntagma**
An exquisite range of elegant, feminine shoes can be found at the boutique store of Greece's Manolo Blahnik. Some of these designs are works of art inspired by '50s and '60s films.

VRAKI *Men's Underwear*
☎ **210 362 7420; Skoufa 50;**
Ⓜ **Syntagma**
As close as you get to a men's lingerie store, quirky Vraki has funky underwear, T-shirt ensembles and casual sportswear. The changing artful window displays and novel

gym lockers and showers in the change rooms are a highlight.

🍽 EAT

🍽 AMADA *Café*   €€
☎ **210 362 2408; Valaoritou 2;**
Ⓜ **Syntagma**
This classy art-deco café on a chic pedestrian café strip off Voukourestiou is a great place for a casual lunch, with gourmet pizzas, salads and snacks and excellent desserts.

🍽 FASOLI *Greek, International* €
☎ **210 360 3626; Ippokratous 22;**
Ⓜ **Panepistimio**
A cheery and great-value new arrival, with quirky platform chairs on the sloping pavement.

Underdressed manequin displaying its unique wares at Vraki

Its menu of salads, pastas and Greek dishes follows the successful formula of its popular sister restaurant in Exarhia.

FILIPPOU *Taverna* €€
☎ 210 721 6390; Xenokratous 19; ⏲ lunch & dinner, closed Sat night & Sun; Ⓜ Evangelismos
Bookings are recommended at this classic taverna in the Dexameni district. It's always packed with locals enjoying the renowned home-style fare. There's a courtyard and tables on the pavement across the road.

OIKEIO *Modern Taverna* €€
☎ 210 725 9216; Ploutarhou 15; ⏲ 8am-11pm Mon-Sat; Ⓜ Evangelismos
With excellent home-style cooking, this cosy modern taverna in a sedate pocket of Kolonaki lives up to its name ('homey'). Try the stuffed zucchini and other good-value traditional dishes.

ORIZONTES
Modern Mediterranean €€€
☎ 210 722 7065; Lykavittos Hill; ⏲ lunch & dinner; 🚕 taxi to funicular
Fine dining with fine panoramic views is the selling point of this elegant upscale restaurant on Lykavittos, with excellent Greek-influenced Mediterranean cuisine.

OUZADIKO
Mezedhopoleio €€
☎ 210 729 5484; Karneadou 25-29 ⏲ lunch & dinner Tue-Sat; Ⓜ Evangelismos
The basement location in the Lemos Centre lets it down, but Ouzadiko is nonetheless cosy and renowned for its refined regional mezedhes, washed down with an ouzo or two from its extensive selection. There are a few tables outside in summer. Bookings advisable.

PAPADAKIS
Seafood, Mediterranean €€€
☎ 210 360 8621; Fokylidou 15; ⏲ lunch & dinner Mon-Sat; Ⓜ Evangelismos
Up in the foothills of Lykavittos, this understatedly chic restaurant specialises in seafood, with creative specialities such as stewed octopus with honey and sweet wine and sea salad (a type of green seaweed/sea asparagus).

TA KIOUPIA
Modern/Traditional Greek €€€
☎ 210 7400150; Dinokratous & Anapiron Polemou 22; ⏲ lunch & dinner Mon-Sat, lunch Sun Ⓜ Evangelismos
Since relocating from Kifisia to this central location, Ta Kioupia has found new fans for its smorgasbord of Greek cuisine, from the islands to the regions, from modern to classic dishes. There is a set menu, as well as à la carte dining.

NEIGHBOURHOODS

KOLONAKI

v

WORTH THE TRIP

For the closest thing to Greek haute cuisine, book a table at **48 The Restaurant** (off map, H5; ☎ 210 645 0658; www.48therestaurant.com; Armatolon & Klefton 48, Ambelokipi; Ⓜ Ambelokipi), the brainchild of much-lauded French-trained chef Christoforos Peskias. Set around an internal courtyard with a pool and cascading water, the restaurant's sleek minimalist design befits its location in the **Ileana Tounta Contemporary Art Centre** (off map, H5; ☎ 210 643 9466; www.art-tounta.gr; admission free; ⏲ 11am-8pm Tue-Fri, noon-4pm Sat; Ⓜ Ambelokipi).

For an after-dinner drink, walk to one of the loveliest garden bars in Athens at **Balthazar** (off map, H5; ☎ 210 644 1215; Tsoha 27 & Vournazou; ⏲ Mon-Sat; Ⓜ Ambelokipi), a glam summer favourite.

DRINK

▼ CITY *Café-bar*
☎ **210 722 8910; Haritos 43;** ⏲ **10am-late;** Ⓜ **Evangelismos**
A popular spot in the small bar strip on the pedestrianised end of Haritos; most nights there are patrons spilling out on to the road, drinking on the steps of the apartment blocks opposite.

▼ FRAME *Bar-restaurant*
☎ **210 721 4368; Dinokratous 1;** Ⓜ **Evangelismos**
In summer, you can chill out with a cocktail on the comfy lounges in the verdant garden of Plateia Dexameni, opposite the main restaurant in the swanky St George Lykavittos Hotel.

▼ MAI TAI *Bar*
☎ **210 725 8306; Ploutarhou 18;** Ⓜ **Evangelismos**

A classic Kolonaki haunt, this atmospheric all-day bar and grill, with a few tables outside on the pavement, attracts an interesting 30-something crowd that gets more boisterous into the evening.

▼ MOMMY *Bar-restaurant*
☎ **210 361 9682; Delfon 4;** Ⓜ **Syntagma**
Just off Skoufa, on the Delfon pedestrian strip, you'll find this trendy retro bar-restaurant buzzing with the cool Kolonaki set who sip drinks on the lounges out on the pavement.

▼ PETIT FLEUR *Café*
☎ **210 681 4825; Omirou 44;** Ⓜ **Syntagma**
Listen to soothing jazz as you sip on your iced tea or a delicious hot chocolate brew at this delightful old-world French-style café. The homey atmosphere and friendly

service is a refreshing break from the Kolonaki glitz.

▼ ROCK'N'ROLL *Bar-restaurant*
☎ 210 721 7127; Loukianou 6 (cnr Ypsilantou); ☾ 9pm-2am, closed summer; Ⓜ Evangelismos

A Kolonaki classic, this upscale club restaurant is rather loud for dinner as it gets very lively. It's known for its Saturday afternoon parties. It's popular with the trendy Kolonaki crowd and has a good vibe. 'Face control' can be strict.

▼ ROSEBUD *Café-bar*
☎ 210 339 2370; cnr Skoufa & Omirou; Ⓜ Syntagma or Panepistimio

One of the more low-key bars with an arty edge, Rosebud is a versatile bar for all occasions and now does food upstairs.

▼ SKOUFAKI *Café-bar*
☎ 210 364 5888; Skoufa 47-49; Ⓜ Syntagma

One of the first to open on Kolonaki's popular bar strip, heading away from the square, Skoufaki is a cosy, arty hangout with good coffee and a friendly upbeat evening crowd.

⭐ PLAY

▣ BARAKI TOU VASILI *Live Music*
☎ 210 362 3625; Didotou 3; ☾ 10.30pm-3am, closed Jun-Sep; admission (incl drink) €13; Ⓜ Panepistimio

An intimate, friendly live-music venue renowned for giving a break to an eclectic line-up of up-and-comers, and occasional touring artists like honorary Cretan, Ross Daly.

▣ DEXAMENI *Cinema*
☎ 210 362 3942; Plateia Dexameni; tickets €7 Ⓜ Evangelismos

This classic open-air cinema is in a lovely spot up on Plateia Dexameni, with a wall of cascading bougainvillea, deck chairs and little tables to rest your beer on.

>METS & PANGRATI

To the east of the Acropolis, opposite the Zappeio Gardens, the residential district of Mets runs behind the imposing Panathenaic Stadium that is built into Ardettos Hill. Mets is an attractive part of old Athens, characterised by some delightful neoclassical and pre-war houses, exemplified on Markou Mousourou – the street leading up to the Athens' First Cemetery and an attraction in its own right. And north up Leoforos Vasileos Konstantinou, modern Greek art is on show at the National Art Gallery.

Northeast of Mets, Pangrati is a diverse residential neighbourhood with interesting music clubs, cafés and old-style family-run tavernas. Plateia Varnava is a great place to experience a typical Athenian neighbourhood, with families dining in the tavernas and kids playing in the square. The main shopping drag is on the streets leading up to and along Ymittou, which has a thriving café strip. Pangrati is a 15-minute walk from Syntagma through the Zappeio Gardens.

METS & PANGRATI

● SEE
Athens' First Cemetery	..1	C6
National Art Gallery	2	A1
Panathenaic Stadium	3	B4
Philatelic Museum	4	B4

⬛ SHOP
Korres	5	B4

🍴 EAT
Alatsi	6	A1
Karavitis	7	A3
Milos	8	A1
Spondi	9	C4
Toula	10	C3
Vyrinis	11	C4

▼ DRINK
Onokio	12	C3

⭐ PLAY
Café Alavastron	13	D3
Exo	14	B5
Half Note Jazz Club	15	B6
Mousikes Skies	16	B3
On the Road	17	B5

NEIGHBOURHOODS

METS & PANGRATI

☾ SEE

☾ ATHENS' FIRST CEMETERY

☎ 210 923 6118; Anapafseos (cnr Trivonianou), Mets; ☾ 7.30am-7pm May-Sep, 8am-5pm Oct-Apr; ☉ 4

In a city with limited open space, the well-tended gardens of the old cemetery are a pleasant, if quirky, place to stroll. The resting places of rich and famous Greeks and philhellenes have some lavish tombstones by leading 19th-century sculptors, including *The Sleeping Maiden* by Halepas and archaeologist Heinrich Schliemann's mausoleum, decorated with Trojan War scenes.

☾ NATIONAL ART GALLERY

☎ 210 723 5937; www.culture.gr; Leoforos Vasileos Konstantinou 50; admission €6.50; ☾ 9am-3pm & 6-9pm Mon & Wed, 9am-3pm Thu-Sat, 10am-2pm Sun; Ⓜ Evangelismos

Greece's premiere art gallery showcases its permanent collection of modern Greek art and hosts major international exhibitions. Exploring the country's art movements, the exhibits include post-Byzantine art and works from the Eptanesian School of secular painters; portraits and historical scenes from the War of Independence and the early years of the Greek state; and leading 20th-century painters. Prize exhibits

Émile-Antoine Bourdelle's sculpture of the *Dying Centaur* (1914), National Art Gallery

Statue of a discus thrower at the Panathenaic Stadium

include three masterpieces by
El Greco.

PANATHENAIC STADIUM
☎ 210 325 1744; www.culture.gr; Vasileos Konstantinou, Mets; Ⓜ Syntagma,
Ⓖ 2, 4, 11
The first modern Olympic Games,
in 1896, were held in the imposing Panathenaic (or Panathenian)
marble stadium, on the site of the
original 4th-century BC stadium
built for Panathenaic athletic
contests. The Romans held gladi-
atorial contests where thousands
of wild animals were slaughtered
and it was later rebuilt by
Herodes Atticus for the Panathenaic Festival in AD 144. The
stadium was completely restored
for the 1896 Olympics and for the

2004 Games. The stadium, which
is known as the Kalimarmaron
(meaning 'beautiful
marble'), made a stunning backdrop to the archery competition
and the marathon finish. Public
access is limited, but it is a site to
behold.

PHILATELIC MUSEUM
☎ 210 751 9066; Fokianou 2, Plateia
Stadiou, Mets; admission free; ⊙ 8am-
2pm; Ⓜ Syntagma, Ⓖ 2, 4, 11
Stamp collectors will love this
small museum, featuring the
history of philately and the post
in Greece, including old mail
boxes, postal uniforms and the
1886 printing plates from the
first stamp, featuring a bust of
Hermes.

NEIGHBOURHOODS

METS & PANGRATI

WORTH THE TRIP

Nestled on the slopes of Mt Ymittos, the 11th-century **Kaisariani Monastery** (off map, D2; ☎ 210 723 6619; Kaisariani; admission €2; ☼ monastery 8.30am-2.45pm Tue-Sun, grounds sunrise-sunset; 🚌) is a peaceful sanctuary only 5km from the city. Athenians once came here to drink from its 'magical' springs. The domed cruciform church, part of a walled complex, has some well-preserved 17th- and 18th-century frescoes. Once the communist stronghold of Athens, Kaisariani is now known for its fine seafood tavernas, clustered on the main square, including the popular **Trata** (☎ 210 729 1533; Plateia Anagenniseos 7-9; ☼ lunch & dinner; 🚌). Behind the church opposite, **Oinothira** (☎ 210 725 8428; Makariou 13; 🚌) has excellent, great value mezedhes and seafood pastas.

SHOP

KORRES *Health & Beauty*
☎ 210 756 0600; www.korres.com; Ivikou 8 (near Panathenaic Stadium), Mets; 🚇 2, 4, 11

You can get the full range from this natural beauty-product guru at the company's original homeopathic pharmacy – at a fraction of the price you'll pay in London or New York.

EAT

ALATSI
Modern Greek €€€
☎ 210 721 0501; Vrasida 13, Ilissia; Ⓜ Evangelismos
Cretan is in, and just behind the Hilton in neighbouring Ilissia, Alatsi represents a new breed of trendy upscale Cretan restaurants, serving traditional cuisine such as wedding pilaf to fashionable Athenians. The food and service are excellent.

KARAVITIS *Taverna* €
☎ 210 721 5155; Pafsaniou 4 (cnr Arktinou), Pangrati; ☼ dinner daily, garden May-Oct; Ⓜ Evangelismos
This no-frills, prewar neighbourhood taverna has a pleasant

Homeopathic products for sale at Korres

garden courtyard and a rustic barrel-filled dining room for winter. The wine is drinkable and the food good value and reliable.

🍴 MILOS
Modern Greek, Mediterranean €€€

☎ 210 724 4400; Leoforos Vasilissis Sofias, Ilissia; ☽ lunch & dinner; Ⓜ Evangelismos

After making its name in Montreal and New York, Milos set up home in the Hilton and established itself as one of the finer fish and seafood restaurants downtown. The quality is superb and the wine list excellent.

🍴 SPONDI
Modern Greek, Mediterranean €€€

☎ 210 756 4021; Pyrronos 5 (off Plateia Varnava), Pangrati; ☽ dinner; Ⓖ 2, 4

This Michelin-rated restaurant in a lovely Athens mansion is one

of Greece's finest restaurants. It has an atmospheric summer courtyard, Mediterranean cuisine, exquisite desserts, faultless service and an excellent wine list.

🍴 TOULA *Ice Cream* €

☎ 210 724 3193; Astydamados 15, Pangrati; Ⓖ 2, 4, 11

You'll be screaming for ice cream from this delectable range of *politiko pagoto* (from Constantinople), including its trademark Mustarda (more toffee than mustard); enjoyed at tables on the square.

🍴 VYRINIS *Taverna* €

☎ 210 701 2021; Arhimidous 11, Pangrati; ☽ lunch & dinner Ⓖ 2, 4, 11 to Plateia Plastira

Just behind the stadium, this popular neighbourhood taverna has had a modern makeover but

Experiencing the delightful, traditional taverna setting at Vyrinis

Christoforos Peskias
Chef, 48 The Restaurant

The dining scene in Athens There are great taverns in Athens. Food has changed in Greece; there are a lot more choices for good modern Greek cuisine. It's based in tradition but uses contemporary techniques. **Recommended for... Fine dining** Varoulko (p84) or Spondi (p127)... **Traditional Greek cuisine** Ouzadiko (p119) in Kolonaki has great traditional food... **Modern Greek cuisine** Athiri (p82); the chef was one of my students... **Summertime** Greeks want a more relaxed environment in summer. They love to b outdoors, dining in a garden or in a square or by the beach. Favourite summe spot Balthazar (p120) is gorgeous in summer. It has one of the loveliest gardens in Athens. It's relaxed and has decent food. You'll see Athenians out on the town and the women all dressed up.

maintains its essence and prices. There's a lovely courtyard garden, simple traditional fare and decent house wine.

DRINK

☎ ONOKIO *Café-bar*
☎ 210 752 2100; Vriaxidos 9, Pangrati; ⓔ 2, 4, 11

With signed Hank Williams posters and busts of Native American chiefs, this incongruous bar is the lovechild of Greece's biggest country and western fan, Nikos Garavelas, who hosts a country-and-western radio show and festival.

PLAY

CAFÉ ALAVASTRON
Live Music
☎ 210 756 0102; Damareos 78, Pangrati; ⏰ 10pm-late Tue-Sat; ⓔ 4

It can feel like there's a band in your lounge room in this intimate, casual world-music bar, which hosts regular appearances by eclectic musicians.

☆ EXO *Club*
☎ 210 923 5818; Markou Mousourou 1, Mets; admission €10 Sun-Thu, €15 Fri & Sat; ⏰ 9pm-late; Ⓜ Syntagma or Akropoli

One of the staples of Athenian summers, this popular nightspot has a great rooftop terrace with views of the Acropolis and Lykavittos Hill. It attracts a hip, mixed-age crowd.

☆ HALF NOTE JAZZ CLUB
Live Music
☎ 210 921 3310; www.half.note.gr; Trivonianou 17, Mets; ⏰ from 10.30pm; Ⓜ Akropoli, ⓔ 2, 11

This is the original and best venue in Athens for serious jazz, with a top line-up playing classic jazz, folk and occasional Celtic music. Book a table, or stand at the bar.

☆ MOUSIKES SKIES *Live Music*
☎ 210 756 1465; Athanasias 4, Pangrati; ⏰ 8pm-late, closed Aug; ⓔ 2, 4, 11

An intimate venue run by a charming singer and bouzouki-player couple with a program of *laïka* (urban pop music), *entekna* ('artistic' music) and *rembetika* (Greek blues), and an arty crowd.

☆ ON THE ROAD *Club*
☎ 210 347 8716; Ardittou 1, Mets; admission €10 Fri & Sat; ⏰ 9pm-late; Ⓜ Syntagma or Akropoli

Located on a traffic island between two busy thoroughfares, this long and narrow bar is a lively option, with guest DJs and the latest club music.

>PIRAEUS

The main port of Athens is a bustling city in its own right, despite having melded into the greater urban sprawl. Most people come here to catch a ferry to the islands, never venturing beyond the intimidating expanse of ferry terminals.

While there are few sights beyond the excellent archaeological museum, Piraeus has its charms, particularly the coastal promenade around its three harbours. The smallest and most picturesque harbour is Mikrolimano (also known as Tourkolimano), where Athenians come to eat at the waterfront fish tavernas and fancier restaurants. Nightlife is concentrated on the cafés and bars on Mikrolimano and around Zea Marina (also known as Pasalimani).

Piraeus' busy downtown commercial centre services the maritime community. The food market and antique stores are located near the metro station, and it's where the colourful Sunday market takes place. The main shopping strip lies around the pedestrian mall on Sotiros Dios. Rising from Mikrolimano is the pretty upmarket residential quarter of Kastella.

PIRAEUS

◉ SEE
Dimotiko Open-Air
Theatre 1 E4
Hellenic Maritime
Museum 2 C6
Municipal Gallery of
Piraeus 3 C3
Pireaus Archaeological
Museum 4 C5

🛍 SHOP
Mandragoras 5 C3
Pireaus Flea
Market 6 C3

🍴 EAT
Cellier Zea 7 C5
Dourambeis 8 F4
Jimmy & the Fish 9 E5

Plous Podilatou 10 E5
Vasilenas 11 B1

🍸 DRINK
Flying Pig Pub 12 B4
Istioploikos 13 E5
Kitchen Bar 14 C6
Pisina 15 D5

Please see over for map

⊙ SEE

⊙ HELLENIC MARITIME MUSEUM

☎ 210 451 6264; Akti Themistokleous, Plateia Freatida, Zea Marina; admission €3; ⊙ 9am-2pm Tue-Sat; Ⓜ Piraeus, then ⬜ 904; ♿

This expansive museum brings Greece's maritime history to life, with models of ancient and modern ships, seascapes by some of Greece's greatest 19th- and 20th-century painters, and guns, flags and maps.

⊙ MUNICIPAL GALLERY OF PIRAEUS

☎ 210 410 1401; Filonos 29; ⊙ 10am-3pm; Ⓜ Piraeus

The gallery's permanent collection of modern Greek art and sculpture has found a new home in the restored historic former post office, with a special section for artists from Piraeus.

⊙ PIRAEUS ARCHAEOLOGICAL MUSEUM

☎ 210 452 1598; Harilaou Trikoupi 31; admission €3; ⊙ 8.30am-3pm Tue-Sun; ⬜ 040 from Syntagma; ♿

Residential apartments flanking Piraeus' picturesque harbour of Mikrolimano

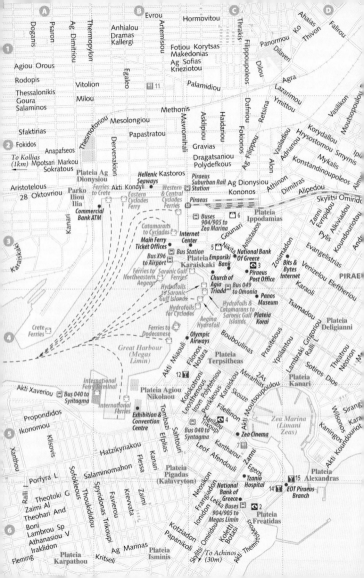

This is a map of Piraeus showing streets, squares, and landmarks.

Streets and locations (labels):

Dogani, Psaron, Ag. Dimitriou, Thermopylon, Evrou, Artemisiou, Hormovitou, Ahaias, Ko, Thivon, Falirou

Anhialou, Dramas, Kallergi, Thrakis, Filippoupoleos, Panormou, Diliaver

Agiou Orous, Vitolion, Egaleo, Fotiou, Korytsas, Makedonias, Ag Sofias, Krieziotou, Dilou, Agra, Vasilikon, Moutsopoulou

Rodopis, Milou, Palamidiou, Dafniou, Lazarimou, Ymittou, Korydallou, Hrysostomou, Smyrnis, Ipi

Thessalonikis, Goura, Salaminos, Mesolongiou, Methonis, Asklipiou, Haidariou, Fokionos, Retsina, Ag Filippou, Vasiladou, Adrianou, Mykalis, Konstantinoupoleos, Alm

Sfaktirias, Papastratou, Mavromihali, Gravias, Dragatsaniou, Polydefkous, Aion, Dimitras, Alipedou

To Kollias (1km) Mpotsari Markou, Anapafseos, Thesmoforiou, Dervenakion, Skylitsi Omiridou, Zaimi, Eripidou, Pyllis

Sokratous, Plateia Ag Dionysiou, Hellenic Seaways, Kastoros, Piraeus Suburban Rail Station, Ag Dionysiou, Kononos, Athinon, Alkiviadou, Koundourioti, Andr

Aristotelous, 28 Oktovriou, Parko Iliou Ilia, Akti Kondyli, Western & Central Cyclades Ferries, Piraeus, Plateia Ippodamias, Evangelistras, PIRAE

Commercial Bank ATM, Eastern Cyclades Ferry, Buses 904/905 to Zea Marina, Gounari, Antichaeos, Zosimadon, Venizelou Eleftheriou

Karaiskaki, Catamarans to Cyclades, Main Ferry Ticket Offices, Internet Center, Bus Station, Bus X96 to Airport, Plateia Karaiskaki, Nikita, National Bank Of Greece, Emporiki Bank, Bits & Bytes Internet, Karaoli

Ferries to Northeastern Aegean, Saronic Gulf Ferries, Church of Agia Triada, Piraeus Post Office, Bus 049 to Omonia, Panos Museum, Tsamadou

Hydrofoils to Saronic Gulf Islands, Hydrofoils & Catamarans to Saronic Gulf Islands, Plateia Korai, Praxitelous, Ypsilantou, Lambraki Grigoriou, Ralli L, Sotiros Dios, Theatrou, Neoron, M

Crete Ferries, Hydrofoils for Cyclades, Aegina Hydrofoil, Ferries to Dodecanese, Olympic Airways, Akti Miaouli, Filonos, Notara, Bouboulinas, Plateia Terpsitheas, Merarhias, 2As, Plateia Deligianni

Great Harbour (Megas Limin), Kolokotroni, Leosthenous, Iroon Polytehniou, Perikleous, Karaiskou, Skouze, Moutsopoulou, Plateia Kanari, Sirang

International Ferry Terminal, Plateia Agiou Nikolaou, Tombazi, Sahtouri, Plateia Pigadas (Kalavryton), Harilaou Trikoupi, Filellinon, Kantharou, Zea Marina (Limani Zeas), Akti Moutsopoulou

Akti Xaveriou, Bus 040 to Syntagma, International Ferries, Exhibition & Convention Centre, Bus 040 to Syntagma, Zea Cinema, Wilsonos, Kara

Propondidos, Hatzikyriakou, Flessa, Kanari, Epfilas, Leof Afendouli, Egeos, Akti Koundouroti

Ikonomou, Klisovis, Salaminomahon, Favierou, Krevvata, Zaimi, Neorion, Tzanio Hospital, Plateia Alexandras

Xanthou, Porfyra L, Sofokleous, Spyridonos Trikoupi, Ionidon, Leka, Frangiadon, National Bank of Greece, Buses 904/905 to Megas Limin, EOT Piraeus Branch

Ralli, Zaimi Al, Theotoki G, Theohari And, Thoukidaidou, Kotziadon, Papanikoli, Koletti Botasi, Plateia Freatidas

Boni, Lambrou Sp, Athanasiou V, Iraklidon, Ag Marinas, Akti Themistos

Fleming, Plateia Karpathou, Kritseli, Plateia Isminis, Skylitsi Omiridou, To Achinos (30m)

WORTH THE TRIP

You can take 3D virtual trips to the galaxy at the state-of-the-art **Planetarium** (off map, H1; ☎ 210 946 9641; www .eugenfound.edu.gr in Greek; Syngrou 387, Palio Faliro; adult/child digital shows €6/3, IMAX €8/5; ⏲ 5.30-8.30pm Wed-Fri, 10.30am-8.30pm Sat & Sun; from Pireaus 🚌, from Syntagma 🚌 B2, 550, E2, E22). Part of the Eugenides Foundation, the 260-seat planetarium has a 950-sq-metre hemispherical dome. To get to the Planetarium from Syntagma, take almost any of the buses along Syngrou to the Onassio stop.

This important museum has stunning antiquities from Piraeus and southern Greece, including finds from a Minoan sanctuary on Kythira. Star attractions are the four colossal bronzes, including a larger than life–sized 520 BC statue of Apollo. A 2nd-century BC theatre has been excavated in the museum grounds.

🛍 SHOP

🛍 MANDRAGORAS *Delicatessen*
☎ 210 417 2961; Gounari 14;
⏲ 7.30am-4pm Mon, Wed & Sat, 7.30am-8pm Tue, Thu & Fri; Ⓜ Piraeus
In the heart of the central food market, this superb delicatessen has one of the finest selections of gourmet delights, from cheeses

and ready-made mezedhes to spices, olive oils and preserved foods to take home.

🛍 PIRAEUS FLEA MARKET
Market
Around Alipedou, Great Harbour;
⏲ 7am-2pm Sun; Ⓜ Piraeus
This busy Sunday market around the streets along the railway line has everything from cheap clothing to tools. For antiques and collectables, you're better off scouring the area's excellent antique shops during the week.

🍴 EAT

🍴 ACHINOS *Modern Greek*   €€€
off map, C6; ☎ 210 452 6944; **Akti Themistokleous 51;** ⏲ lunch & dinner; 🚌
South along the waterfront from Zea Marina, this stylish multilevel place has a great terrace restaurant overlooking the water, with excellent seafood and Mediterranean-Greek menu. There's also a bar below and a café at street level.

🍴 CELLIER ZEA
Mediterranean   €€
☎ 210 418 1049; **Akti Moutsoupoulou 2, Zea Marina;** ⏲ lunch daily, dinner Mon-Sat; 🚌 040 from Syntagma or 🚌 904 from Piraeus metro (Pasalimani stop)
Housed in a neoclassical building overlooking Zea Marina, Cellier has a fine wine store on the

ground level and a restaurant upstairs, with superb views of the harbour from the roof terrace.

☷ DOURAMBEIS
Seafood Taverna   €€€

☎ 210 412 2092; Akti Dilaveri 27;
⌚ lunch & dinner; Ⓜ Faliro

An enduring seafront taverna in Piraeus, this place is popular for fresh fish, grilled to perfection and served with a simple oil-and-lemon dressing.

☷ JIMMY & THE FISH
Seafood, Mediterranean   €€€

☎ 210 412 4417; Akti Koumoundourou 46, Mikrolimano; ⌚ lunch & dinner; 🚗

It's hard to choose between the lobster spaghetti and other sea-food pastas that are house speciali-ties, or the daily catch of fresh fish. One of the more stylish restaurants along Mikrolimano (Small Harbour), Jimmy's has a great range of entrées, including stuffed calamari, and ouzo and sesame prawns.

☷ KOLLIAS *Seafood Taverna* €€
off map, A2; ☎ 210 462 9620; Plastira 3 (Kalokerinou & Dramas), Tabouria;
⌚ lunch & dinner Mon-Sat; 🚗

It's worth risking a clash with an Athenian taxi driver to eat fresh fish and seafood on the terrace of Tassos Kollias' superb taverna in Piraeus' outer reaches. For tighter budgets, you can get five seafood treats for €15 a head across the road at his mezedhopoleio, Ta Pente Piata.

Sample the daily catch at Jimmy & the Fish

🍴 PLOUS PODILATOU

Seafood, Mediterranean   €€€

☎ 210 413 7910; Akti Koumoundourou 42, Mikrolimano; 🕐 lunch & dinner; 🚌 or 🚇 20 from Piraeus metro

The year-round sister restaurant of modern Greek cuisine pioneer, Kitrino Podilato in central Athens, offers elegant dining on the picturesque Mikrolimano harbour, with an emphasis on seafood.

🍴 VASILENAS

Seafood Taverna   €€

☎ 210 461 2457; Etoliko 72; 🕐 dinner Mon-Sat; Ⓜ Piraeus

This classic Piraeus tavern has been spruced up and the menu modernised, but the third genera-tion now running the show main-tains much of the family tradition and well-deserved reputation for good-value, delicious seafood. You can't go wrong with the gen-erous set menu (€34) and there's also à la carte dining (and a few meat dishes) on the shady terrace in summer.

🍷 DRINK

🍷 FLYING PIG PUB *Pub*

☎ 210 429 5344; Filonos 31; 🕐 9am-1am; Ⓜ Piraeus

Run by friendly Greek Australians, the Pig is a popular bar with the shipping crowd in central Piraeus. There's a large range of beers on tap and it also serves decent pub

Dining on seafood at the water's edge at Plous Podilatou

food, including a generous English breakfast.

☫ ISTIOPLOIKOS *Bar-restaurant*
☎ 210 413 4084; Akti Mikrolimanou; €8 Sun-Thu, €10 Fri & Sat; ⏲ 10am-3.30am; 🚌 or 🚎 20 from Piraeus metro

This classy bar-restaurant on a moored, restored ship at the western end of Mikrolimano harbour has great panoramic views. The top-deck bar (a café by day) stays lively until late.

☫ KITCHEN BAR *Bar-restaurant*
☎ 210 452 2338; Zea Marina; ⏲ 10am-late; 🚌 040 from Syntagma or 🚌 904 from Piraeus metro (Pasalimani stop)

Right on the waterfront, this trendy American-style bar-restaurant is OK for a bite to eat, but it's really in its element later in the night, when it turns into a lively bar.

☫ PISINA *Bar-restaurant*
☎ 210 451 1324; Zea Marina; ⏲ noon-1am; 🚌 or 🚌 040 from Syntagma or 🚌 904 from Piraeus metro (Pasalimani stop)

This modern bar-restaurant, set around a pool overlooking the yachts on Zea Marina, is a good choice to cool off with a relaxing drink.

>KIFISIA

Leafy Kifisia is only 10km north, yet a world away from the harsh urban landscape of downtown Athens. Kifisia's tree-lined streets are dotted with high-walled grandiose mansions and 19th-century villas with manicured gardens dating back to the time when it was a summer retreat for the aristocracy; the neighbourhood's location beneath Mt Pendeli (1107m) makes it several degrees cooler than central Athens.

While some areas retain an exclusive old-world feel, a population boom in the last 20 years has given it a more suburban, albeit upscale character. Top fashion labels are amply represented in fancy boutiques and shopping malls in the streets branching east off Kifisias towards busy Plateia Kefalariou (Kefalari Sq). Kefalari has several boutique hotels, predictably pricey cafés, international restaurants and high-end dining options.

Kifisia is the end of the line for the original metro. The botanic gardens, opposite the station, have hosted a major flower show each spring since the 1930s.

KIFISIA

👁 SEE
GAIA Centre 1 D1
Goulandris Natural
   History Museum 2 D1
Mihalarias Art 3 C1

🍴 EAT
Il Salumaio
   D'Atene 4 C2
Semiramis 5 E1
To Berdema 6 C1

Vardis 7 E1
Varsos 8 C2

🍸 DRINK
Mansion 9 E1

👁 SEE

👁 GOULANDRIS NATURAL HISTORY MUSEUM

☎ 210 801 5870; www.gnhm.gr; Levidou 13; adult/child museum €5/3, museum & GAIA Centre €7/4, child under 5 free; 🕑 9am-2.30pm Mon-Sat, 10am-2.30pm Sun, closed Aug; Ⓜ Kifisia

The museum has comprehensive exhibits of animals and plant life, fossils and shells, while the interactive GAIA Centre around the corner focuses on the environment and evolution of the planet. There's an English audio commentary (€2).

👁 MIHALARIAS ART

☎ 210 623 0928; www.mihalarias.gr; cnr Kifisias & Diligianni; 🕑 10am-8pm Tue, Thu & Fri, 10am-4pm Wed & Sat; Ⓜ Kifisia

WORTH THE TRIP

The impressive **Athens Olympic Sports Complex** (OAKA; off map, C4; ☎ 210 683 4777; www.oaka.com.gr; Marousi; Ⓜ Irini) is where the main action took place during the 2004 Olympics. You can wander through the site freely to see Santiago Calatrava's striking glass-and-steel roof and the futuristic shimmering Wall of Nations, but the stadiums are only accessible to organised tours (per person €3; minimum of 15 people), which independent travellers can request to join (fax 210 683 4021).

This top-end gallery, in a stunning heritage-listed building, has paintings and sculpture by leading 19th- and 20th-century Greek and international artists, as well as special exhibitions.

🍴 EAT

🍴 GEFSIS ME ONOMASIES PROELEFSIS *Modern Greek* €€€

off map, C1; ☎ 210 800 1402; Kifisias 317 🕑 dinner Mon-Sat; 🚗

The name means 'flavours with appellation of origin', and this stylish, established restaurant specialises in traditional regional cuisine and produce, with a sophisticated, modern touch. Located in a renovated mansion, the menu is also notable for an excellent cheese and wine selection.

🍴 IL SALUMAIO D'ATENE

Modern Italian, Mediterranean €€€

☎ 210 623 3934; Panagitsas 3; 🕑 Mon-Sat; Ⓜ Kifisia

An offshoot of the Milan original, this very upscale deli-café-restaurant has outdoor seating around a fountain in the shady palm courtyard. The pastas are excellent and deserts divine.

🍴 SEMIRAMIS

Mediterranean €€€

☎ 210 628 4400; Harilaou Trikoupi 48; 🕑 lunch & dinner; Ⓜ Kifisia

Gefsis Me Onomasies Proelefsis (opposite)

Even if you don't spend the night, you can still check out Karim Rashid's out-there design hotel, dining on fine Mediterranean cuisine by the psychedelic amorphous pool.

🍴 TO BERDEMA *Taverna* €€€
☎ 210 801 3853; Vasilissis Amalias 20; 🕐 closed Sun; Ⓜ Kifisia

Tucked in a quiet residential street, this modern taverna with an east-west fusion menu has a delightful garden courtyard. The light-shades made from graters hanging from the trees are part of the playful décor. You can't miss the hotel – look for the pink glass façade.

🍴 VARDIS
Modern French, Mediterranean €€€
☎ 210 628 1660; Deligianni 66, Kefalari; 🕐 dinner Mon-Sat; 🚗

Greece's Michelin-star French restaurant, Vardis is one of the big players in Athens' gastronomic scene. Located in the elegant Pentelikon hotel, it has contemporary French cuisine with exquisite service and wine.

🍴 VARSOS *Patisserie, Café* €
☎ 210 801 3743; Kassaveti 5; 🕐 7am-1am; Ⓜ Kifisia

This huge patisserie has been making traditional sweets and dairy products since 1892. Dine in the old-style café, or sit outside in the courtyard and sample the famous rice pudding, honey pastries, honey or scrumptious cheese pies.

🍸 DRINK
🍸 MANSION *Club-restaurant*
☎ 210 623 3472; Kolokotroni 34, Ⓜ Kifisia

Kifisia is where the money is, and the point is made with no shame at this appropriately ostentatious club restaurant with an over-the-top baroque design.

>GLYFADA & THE COAST

The southeastern coast of Athens is an almost continuous stretch of sandy beach overlooking the Saronic Gulf, stretching about 25km to Varkiza. A scenic tram line follows coastal Leoforos Posidonos from Faliro to Voula, passing promenades, cafés, organised beaches, marinas, playgrounds and some of the most impressive seaside clubs in Europe.

The most popular destination is cosmopolitan Glyfada and its impressive cluster of glamorous beach bars. Once a resort town, Glyfada, 14km from Athens, has now joined with the sprawling seaside suburbs. Lively year-round, it has little to envy about downtown Athens when it comes to shopping. It's popular with expats and its international flavour is partly a throwback from the days when there were American military bases and the old airport nearby. Glyfada is also home to Athens' only golf course.

Beyond Glyfada lies the dramatic stretch of coast often referred to as the Athenian Riviera, dotted with spectacular coves and luxurious beach resorts. See also p18 for more information.

GLYFADA & THE COAST

SEE
Alimos 1 C1
Flisvos Marina 2 C1
Limni Vouliagmenis......3 D2

EAT
Akanthous.......................4 B5
Bakaliko Ola Ta Kala 5 C3

Biftekoupoli-George's
 Steakhouse.................6 B3

DRINK
Rich...................................7 C4

PLAY
Akrotiri Boutique 8 C2
Babae 9 B5

Balux House Project......10 B5
El Pecado Isla................11 C2
Island.............................12 D2
Mao Summer.................13 A3
Vinilio 14 A2

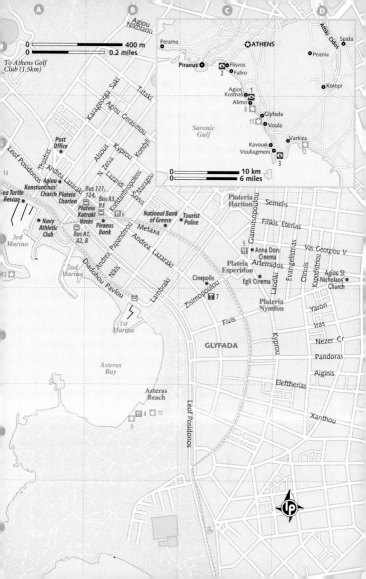

SEE
FLISVOS MARINA
☎ **210 987 1000; www.flisvosmarina .com; Palio Faliro;** 🚊 **4 to Trocadero stop**
For a glimpse at the toys of the privileged class, take a walk around the new Flisvos Marina – Greece's most prestigious VIP mega-yacht parking lot. More than 200 gleaming luxury boats are berthed at the marina, and the impressive seaside redevelopment includes restaurants, cafés and shops. South from the promenade, you can walk along the waterfront to Alimos seaside resort, along the way unleashing your inner child at one of biggest playgrounds in the Balkans.

EAT
AKANTHOUS
Bar-restaurant €€
☎ **210 968 0800; Leoforos Posidonos 58, Asteras Beach; admission €10 Fri & Sat;** 🕙 **10am-late;** 🚊 **5**
One of Athens' more casual beach bar-restaurants, popular with 30-somethings, this excellent mezedhopoleio does a busy dinner trade. After midnight the bar livens up and can turn into a beach party.

BAKALIKO OLA TA KALA
Modern Greek €€
☎ **210 324 7607; Giannitsopoulou 1 (cnr Kyprou);** 🕙 **lunch & dinner Mon-Sat, 5pm-midnight Sun;** 🚊 **5**
This smart deli restaurant offers traditional Greek cuisine and more experimental dishes. There's a range of salads and plenty of Greek gourmet treats to take away.

BIFTEKOUPOLI-GEORGE'S STEAKHOUSE *Taverna* €
☎ **210 894 2041; Konstantinoupoleos 4-6;** 🕙 **lunch & dinner;** 🚊 **5**
Since George's opened in 1951, a row of grill houses serving *biftekia* (tasty Greek burger-cum-meatballs) followed, earning the area the moniker *biftekoupoli* (burgerland). You'll find great-value grilled meats, salads and appetisers here.

WORTH THE TRIP
People swim year-round at quirky **Limni Vouliagmenis** (☎ 210 896 2239; Vouliagmeni; admission €7; 🕙 7am-7.30pm summer, 7am-5pm winter; 🚌 A2 [E2 express in summer] to Plateia Glyfada stop [aka Plateia Katraki Vasos], then 🚌 114), a lake renowned for its constant 22°C therapeutic mineral waters. Tucked in a sheltered rock face, just off Vouliagmeni beach, it's a wonderful setting, with manicured lawns, an old-style café-bar, and a regular crew of elderly citizens in their bathrobes and bathing caps. Part salt-, part spring-water, its source has never been found – divers have lost their lives attempting to discover it.

BEACH BOUND

There are free public beaches along the coast, but most of the better beaches are slick privatised mini-resorts, with admission charges (€6 to €15). Facilities include sun beds, lockers and showers, cafés and bars, while the fancier ones have playgrounds, beach-volleyball facilities, water sports and even cabanas.

 # DRINK

RICH *Bar-restaurant*

☎ 210 898 1710; Zisimopoulou 8; 🍸 5

In the centre of Glyfada's buzzing café and bar strip, flavour of the day is Rich, a sleek multitiered bar with good music and cocktails.

 # PLAY

⚙ BALUX HOUSE PROJECT
Bar-restaurant, Club

☎ 210 898 3577; Leoforos Posidonos 58; admission €15; ⏱ 9.30am-2am; 🍸 5

This cast glass–fronted beach house is an all-day hangout set up as a series of living rooms. The youthful crowd lounges around playing cards, board games or pool, surfing the net, or curled up in a beanbag with a book.

Groovy young things hanging out at the Balux House Project

SUMMER CLUBBING

The glam, pulsating seaside clubs spread along the coast of Athens have to be seen to be believed. Summer is party time and every season there's a new 'hot' club, though often it's only the names, décor and attitude that change. On most nights you'll find a dance party at one of the massive clubs. Renowned for its dance parties, **Akrotiri Boutique** (☎ 210 985 9147; Vas Georgiou B 5, Agios Kosmas, Kalamaki; 🚊 4) is one of the more established mainstream clubs with a fantastic beach setting. The bells were ringing at the summer version of Psyrri's **El Pecado Isla** (☎ 210 895 9645; Karamanli 14, Voula; 🚌) – see also p87 – and the popular **Babae** (☎ 210 894 1620; Leoforos Posidonos 88, Glyfada; 🚊 5), right on the beach, while **Mao Summer** (☎ 210 894 4048; Diadohou Pavlou, Glyfada; 🚊 5) has a massive pool and younger crowd. Further down the coast, all-time favourite **Island** ☎ 210 965 3563/4; Limanakia Vouliagmenis, Varkiza; admission €13; 🕐 midnight-late; 🚌) has romantic white Cycladic-island décor.

Entry to most clubs costs €10 to €15 and be warned, the restaurants are pricey. Many can be reached by tram (24 hours on weekends).

⭐ VINILIO *Nightclub*

☎ 210 968 1056; Leoforos Posidonos 33; 🕐 admission €10 Sun & Tue-Thu, €15 Fri & Sat; 🕐 Tue-Sun; 🚊 5, 🚌

The only dedicated 'disco' in town, this place is packed with tourists and locals of all ages wanting an old-fashioned boogie to '60s, '70s and '80s music. It's in the Emmantina Hotel along the coast, and moves to Varkiza in summer.

>EXCURSIONS

The awe-inspiring Temple of Poseidon, perched dramatically on the edge of Cape Sounion (p148)

CAPE SOUNION

One of the most spectacular ancient sites in Greece, the **Temple of Poseidon** is perched dramatically on the craggy cliffs of Cape Sounion, a scenic coastal drive along the southeast coast of Athens.

Built in the 5th century BC around the same time as the Parthenon, the temple gave great comfort to sailors in ancient times; spotting it meant they were nearly home.

The well-preserved marble Doric columns are impressive from afar but the evocative site also enjoys stunning vistas across the Saronic Gulf and, on a clear day, as far as the Aegean islands and the Peloponnese. Lord Byron waxed lyrical about the place and carved his name into one of the columns in 1810. The site also contains scanty remains of a propylon, a fortified tower, and a 6th-century-BC temple to Athena to the northeast.

In summer, you can stop along the coast nearby for a swim and eat at one of the beachside tavernas, before ascending to the temple in the late afternoon, when people gather to enjoy the breathtaking sunsets.

INFORMATION

Location 70km southeast of Athens

Getting there Inland and scenic coastal bus services leave hourly from Athens' Mavromateon terminal (Map p103, A1; ☎ 210 823 0179; Areos Park, Athens; €5.40), stopping near Syntagma (Map pp40–1, E4) on Filellinon (cnr Xenofontos).

Contact ☎ 22920 39363

Costs Admission €4; free Sun Nov-Mar

When to go ☽ 9.30am-sunset during summer, 9.30am-5pm in winter (best appreciated early morning or late in the afternoon, when most tour buses have gone)

Eating There's a decent on-site café with great views.

DELPHI

An alluring combination of history and mythology, inspiring ruins and a spectacular location make Delphi one of Greece's most fascinating archaeological sites. The ancient Greeks regarded it as the navel of the earth; according to mythology, Zeus released two eagles at opposite ends of the world and they met at Delphi. When you stand on the spectacular plateau, you can't help but feel the potent spirit of the place. Built on the slopes of Mt Parnassos, overlooking the Gulf of Corinth, the **Sanctuary of Apollo** is surrounded by valleys of cypress and olive trees. Pilgrims once came here (around the 4th century BC) seeking the wisdom of Apollo's mystical oracle – thought to be literally the mouthpiece of the god – who delivered her answers in an intoxicating vapour-induced trance. In ancient times the Sacred Way was lined with treasuries and statues given by grateful city-states in thanks to Apollo for helping them win battles.

Ancient Delphi managed to amass a considerable treasure-trove, reflected in the superb collection of finds from the site in the refurbished **museum**, including the celebrated life-sized bronze charioteer, whose piercing eyes follow you around the room. The sprawling site includes the ruins of a **theatre** and well-preserved **stadium**, **pool**, **gymnasium** and **agora**.

If you have your own wheels, the skiing village of **Arahova**, 12km from Delphi, is a good place to stop for lunch. You can also detour down to the quiet seaside village of **Galaxidi** for fresh fish at one of the seafront tavernas (about 30 minutes' drive).

INFORMATION

Location 178km northwest of Athens
Getting there Terminal B (Map p97, B1; ☎ 210 831 7096; Liossion 260, Athens; €13.60, three hours); hire a car or take an organised tour (p189).
Contact ☎ 22650 82312
Costs Admission €9 (including museum); free Sun Nov-Mar
When to go ☼ 7.30am-7.30pm Apr-Oct; 8am-5pm Nov-Mar; museum: 7.30am-7.30pm Apr-Oct; 8.30am-6.45pm Mon-Fri, 8.30am-2.45pm Sat, Sun & public holidays Nov-Mar
Eating In Delphi town, try Taverna Gargadouas (☎ 22650 82488; Vas Pavlou & Frederikis); in Arahova, traditional cuisine at Taverna Agnandio (☎ 22670 32114); in Galaxidi, Taverna Kavouras (☎ 22650 42003) is known for fresh fish normally caught by the owner.

EXCURSIONS

HYDRA

Though there are closer island escapes from Athens, Hydra's (*ee-dhr-ah*) unique appeal has as much to do with the blissful absence of cars and motorbikes as its charming port town.

You can see why the picturesque island is adored by artists and writers as soon as you enter the harbour. Gracious stone and whitewashed mansions on the hillside surrounding the port form a stunning natural amphitheatre.

Idyllic, whitewashed hillside architecture rising from Hydra's harbour

Donkeys and mules – the only means of land transport – greet you in the bustling port that's lined with waterfront cafés and shops. The winding narrow streets and alleyways leading off the port are a good place to get pleasantly lost, passing galleries and boutiques on the way to the town's peaceful and virtually deserted upper reaches.

The splendidly restored **Lazaros Kountouriotis Historical Mansion** (☎ 22980 52421; admission €4; 🕑 9am-4pm Tue-Sun) is a fine example of late 18th-century architecture.

Despite the cruising day-trippers, Hydra is an upscale island, with classy boutique hotels, stunning private homes and prices to match. The rocky outcrop around Hydronetta, near the port, is popular for swimming, or you can take a pleasant walk to some small coves nearby.

Excursion boats or water taxis can take you to further beaches, just ensure they can get you back in time to catch your ferry. Sadly, Hydra suffered badly in the 2007 fires, with much of the forest east of town razed.

INFORMATION

Location Saronic Gulf, 50km (38 nautical miles) from Piraeus

Getting there Several operators run daily high-speed catamaran services, including Hellenic Seaways (Map pp132-3, B2; ☎ 210 419 9000, Athens), which has a 1½-hour service several times daily, while a slower ferry (three to 3½ hours) makes the trip twice daily.

Contact Hydra tourist police (☎ 229 805 2205; www.hydra-island.com)

Costs One way €22

When to go Early in summer – leave early to make the most of the day; check off-peak services.

Eating Family-run Geitoniko (☎ 22980 53615) is popular for classic Greek cooking and its pleasant roof garden, while Isalos (☎ 22980 53845) on the port has excellent coffee and snacks.

History and culture draw travellers, but Athenians are busy redefining themselves and living life. The daily balancing act between tradition and evolution is part of the city's fascinating culture, from the resurgence in Greek cuisine, urban music and contemporary art to the Athenians' penchant for shopping, leisure and entertainment.

Atmospheric Filopappou Hill (p11) is a great spot to watch the sun set, with terrific views of the Acropolis (p10)

SNAPSHOTS

ACCOMMODATION

Athens has a broad spectrum of accommodation options, from opulent luxury and designer chic to small pensions and basic budget hotels. Most travellers prefer to stay around Plaka and the quiet neighbourhoods south of the Acropolis, where there are many small, atmospheric hotels and pensions but few five-star offerings. This is the premier sightseeing neighbourhood and is surprisingly quiet at night.

The majority of luxury hotels are around Syntagma, with the cream of the crop on the eastern side of the square. In the streets just off the Ermou shopping mall, more moderate establishments offer the same convenient location. Around Omonia and Monastiraki, many of the area's run-down hotels have been upgraded and transformed into boutique hotels; however, many of the locations are decidedly gritty, especially at night. Cheaper hotels can be found around the back of Omonia, though the area is not very attractive and some of the more basic hotels have a sleazy element. The major international chains are on Leoforos Syngrou, but they're aimed at business travellers rather than tourists wanting to walk to sites.

Budget travellers will find many small hotels around Athinas, near the market, and around Koukaki and the south side of the Acropolis, where you can still walk to all the major sites and shopping areas.

Up north, Kifisia has some impressive luxury and designer hotels for those not wanting to stay in the centre. In the south along the coast beyond Glyfada, the swanky resort area known as the Athens Riviera offers luxury by the sea.

lonely planet Hotels & Hostels

Need a place to stay? Find and book it at lonelyplanet.com. Over 55 properties are featured for Athens – each personally visited, thoroughly reviewed and happily recommended by a Lonely Planet author. From hostels to high-end hotels, we've hunted out the places that will bring you unique and special experiences. Read independent reviews by authors and other travellers, and get practical information including amenities, maps and photos. Then reserve your room simply and securely via Hotels & Hostels – our online booking service. It's all at lonelyplanet.com/hotels.

Athens hotels underwent a much-needed overhaul in the lead-up to the 2004 Olympics, when new places opened and many older establishments were totally reconstructed. Accommodation improved across the spectrum, with prices rising accordingly.

Greece is in the process of changing its patchy hotel rating method to the five-star international system (many hotels have already adopted it).

Many of the city's hotels are within easy walking distance to a metro station and major sites.

WEB RESOURCES

There are few comprehensive, independent and reliable Greek online accommodation websites for hotels in Athens. An exception is www.greece-athens.com, which has user reviews, direct links to hotel sites and several online booking options. A useful industry-led site with hotel listings, photos and maps (but no independent reviews) is www.gtahotels.com. You can also try the global accommodation standards like www.expedia.com; www.booking.com and www.tripadvisor.com.

BEST DESIGNER HOTELS/ BOUTIQUE HOTELS
> Fresh Hotel (www.freshhotel.gr)
> Periscope (www.periscope.gr)
> Baby Grand (www.classicalhotels .com)
> Semiramis (www.semiramisathens .com)
> Ochre & Brown (www.oandbhotel.com)

BEST ON A BUDGET
> Hotel Exarhion (www.exarchion.com)
> Attalos Hotel (www.attaloshotel.com)
> Athens Studios (www.athens studios.gr)
> Cecil Hotel (www.cecil.gr)
> Tempi Hotel (www.tempihotel.gr)

BEST BANG FOR YOUR BUCK
> Central Hotel (www.centralhotel.gr)
> Hera Hotel (www.herahotel.gr)
> Eridanus Hotel (www.eridanus.gr)
> Magna Grecia (www.magnagrecia hotel.com)
> Park Hotel (www.athensparkhotel.gr)

BEST LAP OF LUXURY
> Hotel Grande Bretagne (www.grande bretagne.gr)
> King George Palace (www.classical hotels.com)
> Electra Palace (www.electra-hotels .com)
> Astir Palace (www.astir-palace.com)
> Pentelikon (www.pentelikon.gr)

FOOD

Greek cuisine is enjoying a renaissance. Postmodern tavernas are all the rage, with a new generation of classically trained chefs redefining the classics to create modern Greek food. These days there's almost haute Greek cuisine (p128), with avant-garde chefs presenting an alternative take on traditional flavours and dishes. Regional cuisine is also coming to the fore, with menus showcasing produce, cheeses and culinary traditions from around Greece, most prominently by the recently fashionable restaurants serving Cretan cuisine.

Traditional Greek food is essentially rustic provincial cooking based on fresh produce and regional ingredients and influences. Simple flavours and minimal dressings bring out the taste of the Mediterranean. While meat has become more prominent in the Greek diet, vegetarians are well catered for as pulses and seasonal vegetables were the mainstay of Greek cooking – made tastier by olive oil.

Greeks love to eat out and dining is a rowdy, drawn out and communal affair with friends and family. Despite the proliferation of upscale trendy restaurants, the most popular dining venue for locals and visitors alike is the trusty taverna.

Athens has many superb casual, family-friendly old-style tavernas, where you can eat well on a moderate budget. Most serve a combination of *mayirefta* (oven-baked or casserole-style dishes) and *tis oras* (made-to-order meat and seafood grills).

A *psistaria* is a taverna that specialises in grilled meats (some specialise to the degree that they only do pork or lamb chops), with a limited menu of salads and starters. The fish and seafood taverna is known as a *psarotaverna*.

Home-style cooking is the speciality of *mayiria* (cook houses), with some of the best traditional places tucked in arcades and in basement haunts around the market and business district, catering to city workers.

The meze-style of dining (usually at a *mezedhopoleio*) is very popular, with dishes shared over long and merry meals – a variation is the *ouzerie*, where ouzo traditionally helped rinse the palate between meze tastes.

Many upscale tavernas merely serve slicker versions of traditional dishes in stylish surrounds (for a much higher bill), so you're often better off sticking to the real thing. Bar-restaurants are still popular, but can get very noisy as the night goes on.

With a few exceptions, most of the restaurants around Plaka and the Acropolis cater to tourists, serving substandard and overpriced predictable fare. Great authentic tavernas can be found in neighbourhoods like Pangrati, Exarhia and Petralona, while Kolonaki has many excellent upscale restaurants. Gazi is the latest dining hotspot, with fine restaurants also opening around Keramikos and Metaxourghio. Piraeus has always been popular for fresh fish at one of the waterfront tavernas, especially on Mikrolimano Harbour.

Athens has no shortage of international-style restaurants and almost any type of ethnic cuisine, from Indian to fancy Michelin-rated French restaurants. With a few exceptions, most Asian restaurants are tame and expensive.

Athens' seasonal dining scene means many restaurants close for the summer, often moving to sister restaurants on the islands. Summer is about alfresco dining in delightful courtyards and cool terraces or pavement tables, or heading to the waterfront.

Be warned, Greeks eat late (tourist-friendly eateries open earlier). Typical dinner bookings are for 9pm to 10pm and it's not uncommon for tables to start filling at midnight. Tavernas are often open all day, so late lunchers are well catered for.

BEST MODERN GREEK
> 48 The Restaurant (p120)
> Athiri (p82)
> Kuzina (p83)
> Mani Mani (p56)
> Alatsi (p126)

MOST ROMANTIC VIEWS
> Varoulko (p84)
> Pil Poul (p83)
> Filistron (p82)
> Orizontes (p119)
> Kuzina (p83)

BEST BUDGET MEALS
> Ariston (p46)
> Thanasis (p73)
> Kostas (p47)
> Fasoli (p118)
> Diporto Agoras (p99)

BEST TRADITIONAL TAVERNAS
> Vyrinis (p127)
> Skoufias (p92)
> Ikonomou (p85)
> Nikitas (p83)
> To Steki tou Ilia (p84)

DRINKING & NIGHTLIFE

Come nightfall, Athens is undoubtedly one of the liveliest European capitals. A heady cocktail of hedonistic Greek spirit, restless energy and relaxed drinking laws contribute to the city's vibrant nightlife. The pursuit of a good time is considered almost sacrosanct – as evidenced some years back when moves to boost the nation's productivity by imposing stricter closing times failed miserably.

Athens' sophisticated bar scene includes anything from glamorous bars and hip arty hangouts to casual neighbourhood haunts. New bars open constantly as fads come and go, the recent hotspots being Psyrri and Gazi, while hip bars are sprouting in the back streets around Syntagma and emerging areas like Keramikos. Alternative music clubs and crowded cheap student bars are found around Exarhia, while Kolonaki's bar scene ranges from the fashionably cool to more laid-back classic haunts.

While mayhem reigns on weekends, weeknights are still surprisingly lively. Bars often don't kick off until 11pm, nightclubs well after midnight and the city's infamous *bouzoukia* (see Music, p161) come alive even later. Most clubs have a door charge and pricey drinks, although the measures are usually doubles.

In summer, the action moves to rooftop terraces and garden courtyards, spills out onto the pavements, or revellers brave the traffic to party at the beachside clubs (see Summer in the City, p160).

While alcohol is freely available, even at the corner kiosk, Athenians don't drink to get off their faces (drinks often come with a snack) and public drunkenness is uncommon and frowned upon.

A favourite Greek pastime is to go for an 'ouzo', w[...]
ing copious carafes of the famous tipple (diluted wit[...]
a drawn-out meal of mezedhes. Retsina is okay for a [...]
to sample the excellent new-generation Greek wine[...]

MOST HIP ALTERNATIVE BARS
> Booze Cooperativa (p47)
> Bartessera (p47)
> K44 (p93)
> Kinky (p74)

MOST ATMOSPHERIC CAFÉS
> Melina (p74)
> Petit Fleur (p120)
> Tristrato (p74)
> Amalthia (p70)

TOP NIGHTCLUBS
> Decadence (p108)
> El Pecado (p87)
> Envy (p87)
> On the Road (p129)

Top left Chatting away at the Blue Train (p92) **Above** Playing it cool at the stylish Lallabai (p49)

SUMMER IN THE CITY

Athens may be hard work during the heat of the day, but when the sun goes down, the city's famous nocturnal energy kicks in and the sultry vibe lends itself to magic summer nights.

The city's squares are a hive of activity, while alfresco dining and drinking takes place on terraces, courtyard gardens and bustling sidewalk cafés. The urban hotspots in downtown Athens are a world apart from the coast, which is the playground for Athenians in summer.

If you think the beaches are crowded by day, the traffic heading to the beachside clubs has to be seen to be believed (at its worst after 2am). Take the tram down instead and join Athenians walking along the coastal promenade, stopping for a cocktail at one of the chic bars by the sea.

If you can't escape to an island, you can still get a taste of island life at Athens' glamorous open-air clubs on the seafront, stretching from Piraeus to beyond Glyfada. The glitzy clubs are where the beautiful people dressed to the max (albeit scantily) show off their tans and party until sunrise.

For a more sedate evening, a delightful way to spend a balmy night in Athens is catching a flick at one of the city's charming open-air cinemas. Enjoy a snack, smoke and drink while watching the latest releases or old classics in cool garden settings or stunning rooftop terraces around town. Unlike most European countries, the Greeks don't dub English-language films (check listings in *Athens Plus* or the *Athens News*).

BEST OPEN-AIR CINEMAS
> Cine Paris (p74)
> Dexameni (p121)
> Thission (p87)
> Zefyros (p85)

BEST SUMMER BARS
> Balthazar (p120)
> Gazaki (p92)
> Exo (p129)
> Soul (p85)
> Lallabai (p49)

BEST BEACH CLUBS
> Balux (p145)
> Mao Summer (p146)
> Island (p146)
> Akrotiri Boutique (p146)

MUSIC

Athens has a thriving live music scene in winter, when you can hear the gamut of Greek music, from the popular soulful Greek blues known as *rembetika* to traditional folk music, ethnic jazz, and even Greek rock, rap and hip hop. Athens' many intimate winter venues (most only operate between October and April) also host an eclectic range of touring indie rock, jazz and international artists. In summer, live music is confined to festivals and outdoor concerts by local artists and touring acts – the 2008 line-up included Madonna, Kylie, PJ Harvey, Kiss, Whitesnake, Nick Cave, Iron Maiden, Gloria Gaynor, Manu Chao and the Sex Pistols.

Popular Greek artists include consummate mainstream performers such as Haris Alexiou, Eleftheria Arvanitaki, George Dalaras, Dimitra Galani and Alkistis Protopsalti. Others worth catching live include Alkinoos Ioannides, Socrates Malamas and Nikos Portokaloglou. Ask around for the best shows in town. Indie rock band Raining Pleasure, boundary-defying vocalist Savina Yiannatou, and ethnic jazz fusion artists like Mode Plagal and Kristi Stassinopoulou, are making inroads in the world music circuit.

Greece's big pop acts put on spectacular shows – look out for Anna Vissi, Despina Vandi, Notis Sfakianakis, Ploutarhos, Mihalis Hatziyiannis and Elena Paparizou.

The mainstays of Athenian nightlife are the *bouzoukia*, glitzy and expensive cabaret-style venues (often referred to as *skyladika* – dog houses – because of the crooning B-grade singers), where women dancing the sinewy *tsifteteli* (belly dance) are showered with expensive trays of carnations and revellers party until sunrise.

BEST LIVE-MUSIC VENUES FOR...
> Rock – AN Club (p108)
> Eclectic/World Music – Alavastron (p129)
> Avant-guarde – Bios (p86)
> Alternative and emerging Greek – Baraki Tou Vasili (p121)
> Bouzoukia (and Greek pop acts) – Iera Odos (p93)
> Jazz – Half Note Jazz Club (p129)

GREAT PLACES TO HEAR REMBETIKA
> Perivoli Tou Ouranou (p75)
> Stoa Athanaton (p101)
> Rebetiki Istoria (p109)
> Kavouras (p108)
> Taximi (p109)

ARCHITECTURE

It's rather ironic that the city revered for its architectural legacy is a modern architectural basket case. Ottoman occupation and centuries of decline left Greece an architectural backwater, and even the few Ottoman elements in the city were destroyed in catharsis after independence.

Neoclassicism dominated the rebuilding of the new capital from the 1830s but architecture and urban planning took a backseat during the city's sudden growth spurts and housing shortages, particularly after WWII. During the '50s and '60s, many fine houses were destroyed to make way for characterless, functional six-storey apartment blocks under the system of *antiparohi*, where landowners were given ready-made apartments in exchange for development rights.

While vernacular and often illegal construction reigned, Athens did produce public and private buildings of architectural merit. Examples of postwar modernism include the Athens Hilton, the Bauhaus US Embassy and the Athens Conservatory. Dimitris Pikionis' pioneering landscaping design around the Acropolis set the tone for the pedestrian promenade, while the metro design is world class.

While many neoclassical buildings have been restored, urban regeneration in recent years has focused on historic prewar buildings such as the Citylink complex (see Attica, p45) and former industrial sites, such as the old gasworks in Gazi, the Athinais former silk factory and the Benaki Museum's Pireos annexe.

Ancient and modern coexist in impressive developments such as the National Bank building on Eolou and the new Acropolis Museum designed by Bernard Tschumi and Michael Photiadis, where glass floors and pylons expose the ancient city.

For more information, see also p179.

BEST OF THE ANCIENT
> Parthenon (see Acropolis, p10)
> Erechtheion (see Acropolis, p10)
> Temple of Athena Nike (see Acropolis, p10)
> Lysikrates Monument (p64)
> Temple of Hephaestus (see Ancient Agora, p17)

NEOCLASSICAL BEAUTIES
> Athens Academy (p44)
> National Library (p44)
> Numismatic Museum (p42)
> National Theatre of Greece (p100)
> Plateia Kotzia (p94)

BEST OF THE NEW
> Athens metro (p42)
> Athens Olympic Sports Complex (OAKA; p140)
> Acropolis Museum (p52)
> Tholos theatre, Foundation for the Hellenic World (p91)
> Benaki Museum Pireos Annexe (p90)

Top left Syntagma metro sign and entrance **Above** Playing in the fresh air atop Areopagus Hill (p62), with a bird's-eye view of the Temple of Hephaestus (p17)

STREET LIFE

Whether it's a product of living in tiny apartments, the mild climate or the inherent social nature of the Greeks, life in Athens takes place on the street. The alfresco culture gives Athens a lively buzz, an intoxicating mix of bedlam and joie de vivre. The endless café strips around town can feel like one big open-air lounge room, the relaxed communal vibe at times reminiscent of a village rather than a big city.

Every afternoon, Athenians are out in force for the enduring *volta* (stroll), from families and lovers walking along the new promenade to packs of idle youths sipping endless frappés.

Public space is blatantly appropriated – from the sidewalks crammed with café tables to the neighbourhood squares that become extensions of the tavernas across the street. Neighbourhood streets are blocked weekly for spirited farmers' markets. Shops spread their wares outside their stores, street vendors wheel carts selling nuts, grilled chestnuts, corn and fruit (depending on the season), and immigrant hawkers lay out their merchandise on the pavements (ducking police along the way).

While Athenian society is becoming increasingly westernised, many traditions endure. Lottery sellers roam around rattling their ticket-poles; old-timers sing along to their old *laternas* (wind-up music boxes); men gather in the Zappeio gardens to play backgammon. In Plaka, shopkeepers congregate leisurely outside their stores, intermittently interrupted by potential customers, while roving gypsy entertainers and beggars try their luck on captive audiences in tavernas and cafés.

There's a slice of Athens life around almost every corner, but you'll see Athens in its element particularly around Thisio and Monastiraki and the closed promenade around the Acropolis.

GALLERIES

Athens' status is unrivalled when it comes to ancient art, but the city has not been on the radar of the global modern art world. One of the less talked about changes in Athens in recent years is the thriving contemporary arts scene. Major new arts venues such as the Benaki Museum Pireos Annexe have led a resurgence in the contemporary visual arts. New hubs for cutting-edge galleries are emerging in Gazi, Keramikos and Metaxourghio, as many galleries shift from nearby Psyrri.

Regular shows by reputable and emerging foreign artists, as well as young and established Greek artists can be seen in new and established galleries around town. While many of the more prominent Greek artists work and live abroad, there seems to be a new creative energy in Athens and many more galleries for local artists to show their work.

The country's pre-eminent gallery, the National Gallery (p124), has a vast collection of work by 19th and 20th century Greek artists, which is starting to attract large sums at London's auctions.

Major local collectors of Greek and international art have invested in the arts, including Dakis Ioannou's Deste Foundation, which hosts a prestigious annual art prize.

Most of Athens' galleries participate in the annual Art Athina (p27) art fair, while the city's first biennial was held in 2007. The National Museum for Contemporary Art is yet to open at its new home in the former Fix brewery, but exhibits at various venues around town.

BEST ART GALLERIES
> National Gallery (p124)
> Athens Municipal Art Gallery (p96)
> Herakleidon (p77)
> Benaki Museum Pireos Annexe (p90)

HIPPEST ART SPACES
> Bios (p86)
> K44 (p93)
> Booze Cooperativa (p47)

LEADING CUTTING-EDGE GALLERIES
> Breeder (p97)
> Ileana Tounta Contemporary Art Centre (p120)
> A.Antonopoulou.Art (p77)
> Rebecca Camhi (p97)
> Gazon Rouge (p97)

SHOPPING

Shopping is a favourite Athenian pastime and the number of stores is rather mind-boggling. Major retail development throughout Athens has seen a swathe of new stores opening downtown and the city's first major shopping mall, launched in the northern suburbs.

The most concentrated high-street shopping is on pedestrianised Ermou, which must have more shoes per square metre than anywhere in the world, as well as most of the leading local, European and global brands. The refurbished Citylink complex houses the Attica department store and is the new gateway to the top international designers and big-name jewellers along Voukourestiou, leading to the chic boutiques scattered around Kolonaki.

Plaka and Monastiraki are the places for souvenir hunters, from kitsch statues and leather sandals to jewellery and antiques. Exarhia is the place for more eclectic shoppers, from comics to goth clothing and vinyl. Kifisia and Glyfada also offer great shopping, in a more relaxed environment.

Greek fashion has recently started to make a showing internationally. Athens hosts an annual fashion week (p28). Leading designers include London-based Paris catwalk darling Sophia Kokosalaki, responsible for the stunning costumes in the Athens Olympics opening and closing ceremonies. Other names to look out for are Vasso Consola, Deux Hommes, Yiorgos Eleftheriades, Angelos Frentzos, Haris & Angelos, Lena Katsanidou, Christoforos Kotentos and Celia Kritharioti.

Sale times (July to August and January to February) offer some great bargains. Haggling is only acceptable (and effective) in smaller, owner-run souvenir and jewellery stores (especially for cash).

BEST SHOPPING FOR...
> Mainstream fashion – Ermou (Map pp78–9, E3)
> Designer fashion – Kolonaki (p115)
> Alternative clothing –Exarhia (p104)
> Street wear – Monastiraki (p67)

MOST INNOVATIVE WINDOW DISPLAYS
> Vraki (p118)
> Ropa Lavada (p117)

BEST FOOD & DRINK
> Cellier (p45)
> Mesogaia (p68)
> Pantopoleion (p97)
> Thymari Tou Strefi (p104)
> Athinas and the market district (p96)

GAY & LESBIAN

While homosexuality is generally frowned upon in Greece, you'd be forgiven for thinking Athens is experiencing a gay epiphany. The gay and lesbian community has certainly become more visible and active in recent years. Since 2005, they've paraded through downtown Athens as part of the annual June Athens Pride festival, while the trendy Gazi area has become a prominent focal point for Athens' gay scene, with a concentration of gay or gay-friendly bars, restaurants and clubs attracting a younger gay crowd.

Some more established, low-key gay bars and clubs are found around Makrygianni, while weekly lesbian events are held in bars around town. There are gay saunas and cinemas around Omonia, a dedicated gay bookstore, a lesbian radio show and even an Athens bear bar, while the secluded southern beach area of Limanakia is an established gay haunt.

Despite general tolerance, a significant closet culture exists, with many married men leading double lives. Few celebrities and media types are openly gay. The brutal 2008 murder of a popular actor, who reportedly met his fate after picking up rent boys around Omonia, sent shockwaves around the country. The tragedy came shortly after a furore erupted over the country's first gay marriages, which tested a legal loophole in Greece's non-gender-specific civil union laws.

In a quirky aside, a legal action to prevent gay and lesbian organisations using the term 'lesbian' was launched in 2008 on the island of Lesvos (where the term originated) by locals objecting to the name being misappropriated, claiming they were the true 'Lesbians'.

BEST GAY VENUES
> Sodade (p93)
> Blue Train (p92)
> Lamda Club (p56)
> Alekos' Island (p85)

BEST GAY WEBSITES
> www.gay.gr
> www.lesbian.gr
> www.gaygreece.gr

GAY FRIENDLY
> Magaze (p74)
> Kanella (p91)
> Sappho (p99)
> Gazaki (p92)

MUSEUMS

Athens is seventh heaven for museum buffs, with endless hours of history and culture to devour. The city's 70-plus state and private museums are dedicated to anything from Greece's ancient treasures to more specialist collections and obsessions ranging from philately to trains.

While Athens' archaeological sites are like an open-air museum, many of the most significant sculptures and sections of monuments are held in museums to protect them from pollution and the ravages of time.

Most of Athens museums have been refurbished in recent years but the most exciting and anticipated arrival is the massive new Acropolis Museum, expected to attract more than two million visitors annually.

You could easily spend a day in the country's foremost museum, the National Archaeological Museum, which has the world's most important collection of Greek antiquities.

On the other side of town you can take a journey into Greece's diverse history along Athens' museum avenue, Leoforos Vasilissis Sofias. Starting from the must-see Benaki Museum, along this 1km stretch you'll find stunning mansions housing some of the finest museums.

You'll find another concentration of fascinating small museums, including many folk museums, in Plaka, with the rest scattered around Athens and surrounding areas.

Bear in mind the top museums open later, especially in summer, but smaller museums often close by 2pm – and many are closed on Monday. The Benaki has pioneered evening museum visits, staying open until midnight on Thursday, and other museums have followed suit.

MUST-SEE MUSEUMS

> National Archaeological Museum (p104)
> Acropolis Museum (p52)
> Benaki Museum (p111)
> Museum of Cycladic & Ancient Greek Art (p114)
> Byzantine & Christian Museum (p111)

BEST MUSEUM CAFÉS

> Benaki Museum (p111)
> Islamic Art Museum (p80)
> Numismatic Museum (p42)
> Museum of Cycladic & Ancient Greek Art (p114)

Enjoy spectacular views of the dense city landscape and beyond from Lykavittós Hill (p111)

BACKGROUND

HISTORY

Athens is a city with an epic history spanning more than 3000 years and an unsurpassed and enduring cultural legacy.

Revered as the cradle of western civilisation, Athens was the place of the ancient gods and legends, the city where great philosophers like Plato and Aristotle debated in the Agora and Socrates was sentenced to death for corrupting the minds of Athenian youths. It was the birthplace of democracy, home to the first university and the zenith of architectural and artistic achievement, from the magnificent Parthenon to the great tragedies of Athens' Golden Age, still performed in theatres today.

But Athens' past is also blotted by tumultuous centuries of war, foreign occupation, poverty and political upheaval. By the time it was chosen as the new Greek capital in 1834, it was little more than a dusty outpost of the Byzantine Empire.

Athens carries the scars of its turbulent past and the consequences of its hasty development into a European capital. Ironically Europe's oldest city is also one of its youngest, and still very much a work in progress.

ANCIENT ATHENS

The Acropolis drew some of Greece's earliest neolithic settlers. By 1400 BC it had become a powerful Mycenaean city whose territory covered most of Attica. By the end of the 7th century BC, Athens was the artistic centre of Greece. Athens was ruled by aristocrats and tyrants until Solon, the harbinger of democracy, became *arhon* (chief magistrate) in 594 BC,

ATHENS MYTHOLOGY

Athenian history is steeped in myths and legends. Athena, the goddess of wisdom, became the city's patron deity after winning a contest with Poseidon, god of the sea. King Kekrops, the founder and first king of Athens, had declared that the honour would be given to whoever gave the city the best gift. Athena produced an olive tree, providing oil, food and wood. The sea god Poseidon struck a rock with his trident producing a spring, but it turned out to be saltwater. Another version has a horse leaping out of the spring. Either way, Athena won. The showdown is said to have taken place on the Acropolis (p10) on the sacred site of the Erechtheion temple, notable for its maiden columns known as the Caryatids.

introducing sweeping social and economic reforms that paved the way for democracy, including declaring all free Athenians equal by law and establishing a popular assembly of 400 citizens.

In 490 BC, the Persian army reached Attica but was humiliatingly defeated in the Battle of Marathon (the modern marathon stems from the legend of the messenger who ran 42km from Marathon to Athens to announce the victory before collapsing dead on the spot). Ten years later the Persians returned with a massive army and virtually burned Athens to the ground.

CLASSICAL AGE

Athens reached its Golden Age under Pericles' leadership (461–429 BC), when the treasury moved from Delos to Athens. An illustrious rebuilding program transformed the city – the centrepiece being the Parthenon and the magnificent city of grand temples built on the Acropolis. Athens experienced an unprecedented era of cultural, artistic and scientific achievement, becoming the cultural and intellectual capital whose influence spread beyond Greece. The elegant temples built during this time were the pinnacle of architectural brilliance and an enduring symbol of power.

However, Athens' expansionist ambitions eventually sparked the Peloponnesian Wars, in which Athens suffered badly. During the first war (431–421 BC) a plague broke out, killing a third of the city's population, including Pericles. After Athens surrendered to Sparta in the second war, its fleet was confiscated and the Delian League, the alliance of Greek city-states formed to defend against the Persians, was abolished.

HELLENISTIC PERIOD

The northern kingdom of Macedon led by Philip II emerged as the new power in 338 BC. After Philip's assassination, his son Alexander (the Great) became king and by the end of the 3rd century BC had spread Hellenism into Persia, Egypt and parts of India and Afghanistan.

Alexander treated Athens favourably. His tutor Aristotle taught at the Athens Lyceum. But an unsuccessful bid for independence after Alexander's death led to an intermittent period of subjection to Macedon, although the city's institutions were upheld.

ROMAN RULE

Athens was defeated by Rome in 189 BC after it backed an enemy of Rome in Asia Minor, but the city escaped lightly as the Romans had great respect for Athenian scholarship and supported the teachings of Athenian philosophers. After a second ill-fated rebellion, the Romans destroyed the city walls and carted off many of its finest statues to Rome.

Athens received a pardon from Julius Caesar and, for the next 300 years, it experienced an unprecedented period of peace – the Pax Romana – and became the seat of learning, attracting the sons of rich Romans. During this period Roman emperors, particularly Hadrian, graced Athens with many grand buildings, including the territorial arch marking his turf (p39).

BYZANTINE EMPIRE

With the rise of the Byzantine Empire, which blended Hellenistic culture with Christianity, the Greek city of Byzantium (renamed Constantinople in AD 330, present-day İstanbul) became the capital of the Roman Empire.

The Byzantine Empire outlived Rome, lasting until the Turks captured Constantinople in 1453. Christianity was made the official religion of Greece in 394, and worship of Greek and Roman gods was banned.

Athens remained an important cultural centre until 529, when the teaching of 'pagan' classical philosophy was forbidden in favour of Christian theology. From 1200 to 1450, Athens was occupied by a succession of opportunistic invaders – Franks, Catalans, Florentines and Venetians.

OTTOMAN RULE

In 1456 Athens was captured by the Turks. They ruled Greece for the next 400 years, during which the Acropolis became the home of the Ottoman governor, the Parthenon was converted into a mosque and the Erechtheion was used as a harem. Athens enjoyed a privileged administrative status and a period of relative peace ensued, with some economic prosperity from trade, particularly with the Venetians.

Conflict between the Turks and Venetians led the Venetian general Morosini to lay siege to the Acropolis for two months in 1687, briefly interrupting Turkish control of the city. During this campaign, the Parthenon was blown up when Venetian artillery struck gunpowder stored inside the temple.

INDEPENDENCE

On 25 March 1821 the Greeks launched the War of Independence, declaring Independence in 1822, but infighting twice escalated into civil war, allowing the Ottomans to recapture Athens. The western powers stepped in and destroyed the Turkish-Egyptian fleet in the famous Bay of Navarino.

Initially, the city of Nafplio became Greece's capital. After elected president Ioannis Kapodistrias was assassinated in 1831, Britain, France and Russia declared Greece a monarchy. The throne was given to 17-year-old Prince Otto of Bavaria, who transferred his court to Athens – which became the Greek capital in 1834.

At the time, Athens was little more than a sleepy village of 6000, many residents having fled after the 1827 siege. Bavarian architects created a city of imposing neoclassical buildings, tree-lined boulevards and squares. Otto was overthrown in 1862 after a period of discontent, during which there were power struggles, military and external interventions, including British and French occupation of Piraeus aimed at quashing the 'Great Idea', Greece's doomed expansionist goal. The new imposed sovereign was Danish prince William from the Glücksburg dynasty, crowned Prince George in 1863. The Greek monarchy has retained its Danish links ever since.

WWII & THE GREEK CIVIL WAR

Athens enjoyed a brief heyday as the 'Paris of the eastern Mediterranean' before WWI. A disastrous Greek attempt to seize former Greek territories in southern Turkey, known as the Asia Minor catastrophe, ended with the Treaty of Lausanne in July 1923.

Athens' population virtually doubled overnight as more than one million Greeks were forced out of Turkey in a population exchange. Athens fared badly during WWII, when Germany occupied most of Greece. But more Athenians died from starvation than at the hands of the enemy. When the war ended, fighting between communist and monarchist resistance groups led to a bitter civil war that ended in October 1949, leaving the country a political, social and economic basket case.

Greece faced a mass exodus as almost a million Greeks migrated to the USA, Canada and Australia. In Athens, a mammoth reconstruction and industrialisation program prompted another population boom, as people from the islands and rural villages moved to the city.

COLONELS, MONARCHS & DEMOCRACY

In 1967, right-wing army colonels (the junta) launched a successful military coup. In their ensuing seven-year reign, they curbed civil rights, banned political parties and trade unions and jailed opponents, while many dissidents went into exile.

On 17 November 1973, tanks stormed a student sit-in at Athens Polytechnio (Technical University) to quell a student occupation calling for an uprising against the US-backed junta. While the number of casualties is still disputed (20 students were reportedly killed), the act spelt the death knell for the junta. Its downfall finally came after a disastrous attempt to topple the Makarios government in Cyprus provoked a Turkish invasion of the island.

Democracy returned to Greece in 1974, after a referendum abolished the monarchy. Greece became a parliamentary republic with a president as head of state. The exiled former royal family still lives in London, where it continues to use its royal titles. A dispute between the former king, Constantine, and the government over the family's assets was settled in 2002 and the former royal family members now often return to Greece as private citizens.

PEACE, POLITICS & PROSPERITY

The decades since 1975 have seen an unprecedented period of peace – and drastic social and economic changes as Greece fast-tracked its development into a modern nation. When Greece became the 10th member of the EU in 1981, it was the smallest and poorest member. That same year, Andreas Papandreou's PASOK party was elected Greece's first socialist government. PASOK ruled for almost two decades (apart from 1990–93) until its defeat by the conservative New Democracy party in 2004, under the leadership of Konstantinos Karamanlis. The most dramatic changes in Athens occurred in the lead-up to the successful staging of the 2004 Olympics, when billions were poured into the city's redevelopment.

ANTIQUITIES STRUGGLES

Greece's turbulent history has seen many of its ancient treasures destroyed by bombs and pilfered by foreigners. During WWII, the National Archaeological Museum (p14) became German army offices (and was bombed) and was used as a prison during the ensuing civil war. Thankfully, gold treasures and smaller pieces had been removed and hidden in the vaults of the Bank of Greece, while larger pieces were buried in sand in the bowels of the museum.

Greece entered the European Economic and Monetary Union in January 2002, the drachma making way for the euro. The Greek economy has been in relatively good shape since and the standard of living has risen drastically. The past decade has also seen the influx of nearly one million immigrants and refugees, which is changing the city's demographics and presenting new challenges.

LIFE AS AN ATHENIAN

New shops are constantly sprouting and teeming, the endless sidewalk cafés always abuzz, and in the evening Athenians are out in force eating with friends and family as the city's famous nightlife gets into full swing. No wonder many visitors are left wondering when anyone works in this city. For all of Athens' angst, traffic and chaos, this is a leisure society and, on the surface at least, Athenians have never had it so good.

Athens has become a more cosmopolitan and conspicuously wealthier society in the past 20 years, as the city's population grew to 3.7 million. Urban regeneration has continued since Athens' drastic makeover for the 2004 Olympics. Athenians commute on the efficient metro system, new roads and transport networks have eased the traffic horror, and the city has become a more efficient and functional capital, though arguably still a case study in organised chaos.

Greeks have a work-to-live attitude to life and are prone to displays of excess in dining and entertainment. While Athenians complain about the rising cost of living since the euro, they've embraced consumerism (and credit cards) with gusto and flaunt their new-found wealth, from designer clothes to the latest mobile phones and flashy cars. As though they've been left behind for long enough, Athenians are embracing all that is modern and new.

Athens is one of the most expensive European cities, despite wages being among the EU's lowest. Like their city, Athenians are a paradox – laid back, yet inherently conservative, as hospitable as they can be rude, friendly yet suspicious and conspiratorial, always in a hurry on the road, yet able to linger for hours in cafés. Some hold down double jobs, while others seem to belong to an inexplicably large idle class. Athens' high-density neighbourhoods still maintain a village feel, where small family businesses are the mainstay.

In summer, the city is abandoned en masse as people head to islands and ancestral villages, returning when schools start in September.

LOCAL ETIQUETTE

Despite their often surly demeanour (think shop assistants and public servants), most Athenians are friendly and helpful to visitors. Greeks are proud of their country and respond positively if they see people enjoying it or attempting to speak Greek.

The Greek reputation for hospitality is not a myth, it's just harder to find in a big and self-absorbed city like Athens. Greeks are generous hosts and if you're invited out, the bill is not normally shared – insisting can insult your host, though you should always offer.

Greeks are opinionated and curious; personal questions are not considered rude and few subjects are off-limits, from your how much you earn to why you don't have children. Greeks love to drink, but it's usually with food and they rarely over-imbibe – drunk and disorderly behaviour is frowned upon.

Many Greeks still take an afternoon siesta, so keep the noise down in residential areas between 2pm and 5pm.

The majority of the population belong to the Greek Orthodox Church and the year revolves around the festivals of the church calendar.

Athens has always been a melting pot of Greeks, from the refugees from Asia Minor to the postwar arrivals from Greece's poverty-stricken villages and islands. The latest wave of foreign economic immigrants is changing the city's demographics – the new Athenians include more than 600,000 immigrants from Albania, Poland, India, Pakistan and the Philippines.

ARTS

The distinction between ancient and modern Greece reflects the lack of continuity in Greece's turbulent history – resulting in a virtual cultural black hole between the achievements of ancient Greece and the 19th century, when the modern Greek state was formed.

FINE ARTS

Generations of artists have been influenced by the ancient Greeks, whose sculptures take pride of place in the world's great museums. The primitive prehistoric Cycladic figures have influenced artists like Picasso and Modigliani. In the classical period, artists represented the human figure as true to nature, rather than flat and stylised, for the first time – a typical example being the enigmatic *kouroi* (youths) at the National Archaeological Museum (p104). The realism continued into the Hellenistic period, inspiring artists such as Michelangelo.

The intricate painted terracotta pots of ancient Greece, buried throughout Greece over millennia, give some insight into the extraordinary tradition of ancient pictorial art, also displayed on Minoan frescoes.

Byzantine and Christian art dominated the years before Independence, when 19th-century artists began forging a new Greek artistic identity and were influenced by international art movements.

DRAMA & THEATRE

Drama dates back to the contests staged in Athens during the 6th century BC for the annual Dionysia Festival. At one contest, Thespis left the ensemble and took centre stage for a solo performance, an act considered to be the first true dramatic performance – hence the term 'thespian'. The works of ancient Greek playwrights such as Aeschylus, Sophocles, Euripides and Aristophanes are still performed in the few surviving ancient theatres during summer festivals, most notably at the Odeon of Herodes Atticus (p21) and at Epidavros in the Peloponnese.

Athens supports a lively winter theatre tradition, with more than 200 theatres (more theatres than any other European city) presenting anything from Sophocles to Becket and works by contemporary Greek playwrights.

LITERATURE

The enduring legacy of Greece's literature goes back to Homer, the first and greatest ancient Greek writer, whose tales of the Trojan War and Odysseus' wanderings are told in his epics, the *Odyssey* and the *Iliad*, written in the 9th century BC.

SHINING STAR

One of Athens' most beloved daughters was the charismatic late actress and politician, Melina Mercouri, whose iconic photo, waving on the Acropolis, adorns the Akropoli metro platform. Mercouri achieved international stardom in the '60s and '70s in a string of movies by French director (and later husband) Jules Dassin, and appeared on Broadway. Best remembered as the happy-go-lucky prostitute in *Never on a Sunday* (1960), the outspoken political activist was forced into exile in the junta era. She later became the MP for Piraeus and, in the '90s, a dynamic culture minister, lobbying for the return of the Parthenon marbles. A cultural foundation and quaint café, Melina (p74), are dedicated to her in Plaka.

FURTHER READING

> *Athens* (Michael Llewellyn Smith, 2004) – engaging cultural and literary history.
> *Athens by Neighbourhood* (Diane Shugart, 2001) – colourful local insight into the city.
> *Dinner with Persephone* (Patricia Storace, 1996) – enduring snapshot of the author's year in Athens.
> *Eurydice Street* (Sofka Zinovieff, 2004) – poignant observations on contemporary Athens society.
> *Les Liaisons Culinaires* (Andreas Staïkos, 2001) – mouth-watering tale of culinary seduction in an Athens apartment block.
> *The Late-night News* (Petros Markaris, 2004) – part of the great crime series exploring Athens' underbelly.
> *The World of the Ancient Greeks* (John Camp and Elizabeth Fisher, 2002) – in-depth look at the Greeks' imprint on politics, philosophy, the arts, medicine and architecture.

Herodotus, Thucydides and Plutarch were the first historians, while Pausanias was one of the earliest travel writers. Pre-eminent ancient Greek poets included Pindar, Sappho and Alcaeus.

Celebrated 20th-century poets include Constantine Cavafy and Yiannis Ritsos, and the two Nobel Prize laureates, Giorgos Seferis (1963) and Odysseus Elytis (1979).

Controversial Nikos Kazantzakis, author of *Zorba the Greek* and *The Last Temptation*, remains the most celebrated 20th-century Greek novelist.

Contemporary Greek literature is flourishing and translations are increasing, including the works of acclaimed authors such as Apostolos Doxiadis, Kostas Mourselas and Maro Douka.

MUSIC

While Athens has a thriving indigenous music scene, few contemporary artists or pop acts have made it big internationally. Exceptions from the past include opera diva Maria Callas, living legend Mikis Theodorakis, composer Manos Hatzidakis, and '70s icons Vangelis, Demis Roussos and Nana Mouskouri.

The talented new generation of musicians is making an impact on the world music scene, including vocal artist Savina Yannatou and ethnic jazz acts like Mode Plagal. Revivalist groups are breathing new life into traditional music. Athens has many popular *rembetika* clubs (referred to as the Greek blues), while *entehni* (artistic, or quality) music is doing its best to counter the western-style pop and dance influence.

ARCHITECTURE

Ancient Greek temples remain potent symbols of democracy and architectural brilliance, having inspired major architectural movements such as the Italian Renaissance and the British Greek Revival.

While Greece's architectural legacy includes Minoan, Cycladic, Mycenaean, Archaic, Hellenistic and Byzantine styles, most of the ancient temples in Athens were built in the classical age – characterised by the Doric, Ionic and Corinthian order of columns. The Parthenon (p10) is the pre-eminent example of a Doric temple, while the neighbouring Temple of Athena Nike and the Erechtheion are built in the Ionic style. Ornate Corinthian columns were popular with the Romans, as seen in the Temple of Olympian Zeus (p43).

Byzantine architecture is exemplified by churches built in a cruciform design, with a central dome, and patterned external brickwork. Stylistic frescoes and mosaics symbolically work down from Christ in the dome, to the Virgin in the apse and descend to walls decorated with saints, apostles and Bible scenes.

Little Ottoman architecture survives in Athens, much of it systematically destroyed after Independence. Athens was rebuilt in the neoclassical style to evoke past glory, best exemplified by the grandiose trilogy of the National Library, Athens University and Athens Academy (p44).

Many neoclassical buildings were destroyed in the untamed expansion of the 1950s, '60s and '70s, when the ugly apartment blocks that characterise the modern city were erected. Innovation and architectural merit has largely taken a back seat to pragmatism and haphazard urban

SHOT IN ATHENS

The Acropolis stars in its first Hollywood film after Greek-Canadian actor Nia Vardalos *(My Big Fat Greek Wedding)* got unprecedented permission to shoot the romantic comedy *My Life in Ruins* (2008) on the sacred rock. Noteworthy films set in Athens include Michael Cacoyannis' classic *Never on a Sunday* (1960), shot in Piraeus, and, more recently, Tassos Boulmetis' *Politiki Kouzina (A Touch of Spice*, 2003), about Greek refugees from Istanbul in 1960s Athens. Constantinos Giannaris takes a harsher look at contemporary city life in *From the Edge of the City* (1999) and *Dekapentavgousto* (2001), while up-and-coming Renos Haralambidis presents a lighter view in *Cheap Smokes* (2000). The quirkiest film shot in Athens, however, must surely be the hilariously bad, camp sci-fi parody *Attack of the Giant Moussaka* (2000).

BACKGROUND

OLYMPIC GAMES

The 2004 Olympics left a lasting legacy: Athens today is indeed a radically different city, a more attractive, cleaner, greener and more efficient capital with a modern airport, an expanding metro system, new roads and infrastructure and a renewed sense of civic pride. Ugly billboards were torn down, building façades painted, and the city's spruce-up and regeneration continues, albeit at a slower pace. The showpiece Olympic stadium complex hosts major sporting events and concerts for headline acts like Madonna and Bjork, the badminton venue stages musicals such as *Mamma Mia!* and the rest of the stadiums and venues are (very) slowly being turned into shopping malls, arts and entertainment venues, government offices, a university campus and a water park.

development, though recent years have seen a significant shift and more promising outlook.

For more information, see p162.

ENVIRONMENT

Athens lies in a basin surrounded by hills, opening onto the Saronic Gulf. This topography contributes to the dreaded *nefos*, the blanket of smog that still plagues the city, though to a lesser degree following efforts since the 1990s to reduce vehicle and industrial pollution, including restrictions on vehicles in the centre, better public transport, the gradual abolition of leaded petrol and tougher laws.

Athens was significantly cleaned up before the 2004 Olympics. Millions of trees and shrubs were planted in an attempt to increase green space, though it barely made a blip on the concrete sprawl. The city can still be stiflingly hot on still summer days.

Greece is slowly becoming environmentally conscious. Recycling bins are becoming more common, but Athens has yet to solve major landfill problems.

DIRECTORY
TRANSPORT
ARRIVAL & DEPARTURE
AIR

Athens' **Eleftherios Venizelos International Airport** (☎ 210 353 0000; www.aia
.gr; code ATH) lies near Spata, 27km
east of Athens.

The fastest way to and from the
airport is by metro or suburban
rail. Express buses and taxis are
cheaper but you're at the mercy
of traffic conditions. Express buses
and the suburban rail also connect
with the port of Piraeus.

Athens' airport has great
shopping and services and a
small museum, on the departure
level, displaying archaeological
finds unearthed during airport
construction.

BOAT

Ferries and high-speed catamaran
or hydrofoil services to nearby
islands leave from the port of
Piraeus.

Weekly ferry schedules are
available from tourist offices or
online at the **Greek Travel Pages** (www
.gtp.gr) and you can book online at
Greek Ferries (www.greekferries.gr).

Hellenic Seaways (☎ 210 419 9000;
www.hellenicseaways.gr; ☉ 8am-8pm
Mon-Fri, 8am-4pm Sat & Sun) has regular
services and takes credit-card
bookings.

TRAVEL DOCUMENTS
PASSPORT

You need a valid passport to enter
Greece (or ID card for EU nationals) and to check in at a hotel or
pension.

GETTING AROUND

Central Athens is compact and
relatively pedestrian-friendly and
most of the major sites, shopping,
restaurant and bar precincts can
be reached on foot, which is the
best way to explore the city.

The metro has made getting
around the centre of Athens a relative breeze. It is efficient, clean and
easy to navigate. To get further

CLIMATE CHANGE & TRAVEL

Travel – especially air travel – is a significant contributor to global climate change. At Lonely
Planet, we believe that all travellers have a responsibility to limit their personal impact. As a
result, we have teamed with Rough Guides and other concerned industry partners to support
Climatecare.org, which allows travellers to offset the greenhouse gases they are responsible
for with contributions to sustainable travel schemes. Lonely Planet offsets all staff and author
travel. For more information, check out www.lonelyplanet.com.

afield, you can use the integrated public transport network of buses, trolleybuses (electric cable buses) and the suburban rail and tram. A €0.80 ticket can be used on the entire transport network (except airport services) for 90 minutes.

Athens Urban Transport Organisation (☎ 185; www.oasa.gr; ⏲ 6.30am-11.30pm Mon-Fri, 7.30am-10.30pm Sat & Sun) provides handy directions and timetable information over the phone, while the website has route details and maps.

TRAVEL PASSES

The daily €3 ticket and weekly €10 ticket have the same restrictions on travel to the airport, and it takes a fair amount of travel to make these worthwhile.

METRO

The **metro** (www.amel.gr) runs from 5.30am to just after midnight, every three to 10 minutes depending on the time of day. On Friday and Saturday trains run until around 2am. All stations have wheelchair access. Tickets (€0.80) must be validated at platform entrances and are valid for 90 minutes on all modes of transport.

SUBURBAN RAIL

A fast and comfortable **suburban rail** (☎ 210 527 2000; www.proastiakos.gr in Greek) connects Athens with the airport and the outer regions all the way to Kiato in the Peloponnese. It connects to the metro at Larisis, Doukissis Plakentias and Nerantziotissa.

Travel to/from the Airport

	Taxi
Pick-up point	Outside arrivals hall
Drop-off point	Syntagma
Duration	35min
Cost to centre	€25-30, including freeway tolls (€2.70), airport surcharge (€3.20) and baggage surcharge (€0.32 cents for each piece of luggage over 10kg)
Frequency	n/a
Contact	n/a

The suburban rail can also take you from the airport to Piraeus, changing trains at Nerantziotissa.

TRAM
Athens' single **tram** (www.tramsa.gr in Greek) line takes a scenic route along the coast, but it is not the fastest means of transport. It's handy for revellers travelling to the city's beaches and beach clubs (operating around the clock from Friday evening to Sunday, every 40 minutes).

The central terminus (Map pp40–1, E3) is opposite the National Gardens. Tickets (€0.80) are purchased on the platforms. Trams run from Syntagma to Faliro (☎ 4, 44-50 minutes) and to Voula (☎ 5, 59-65 minutes) from 5am to midnight Monday to Thursday and Sunday and 24 hours Friday and Saturday.

TROLLEYBUS
Athens' overhead cable trolleybuses run between 5am and midnight and service much of the city. Trolleybuses run 24 hours on the 11–Patisia–Pangrati route.

Tickets (€0.80) can be purchased at transport kiosks or most *periptera* (kiosks) and must be validated on board. They are valid for 90 minutes on all modes of transport.

BUS
The **Athens Sightseeing Public Bus Line Route 400** (☎ 185; www.oasa.gr; tickets €5) covers 20 key locations

Metro	Suburban Rail	Bus
Station outside, across from arrivals hall	Station outside arrivals hall	Outside arrivals hall – bus X95
Monastiraki or Syntagma for downtown Athens (or any stop along line 3)	Doukissis Plakentias (for line 3 connection) or Nerantziotissa (for line 1 connection)	Plateia Syntagma; on Othonos
38min	38min	45-50min
€6 (or €10/15 for two/three passengers); valid on all forms of transport for 90min	€6 (or €10/15 for two/three passengers)	€3.20, valid 24 hours on all transport
Every 30min leaving Egaleo between 5.30am and 10.52pm and the airport between 6.30am and 11.30pm	Every 15-20min to Nerantziotissa; to the airport from 6.23am-11.30	Every 15-20min
www.amel.gr	www.proastiakos.gr in Greek	www.oasa.gr

DIRECTORY

in Athens, from the Archaeological Museum to the markets and ancient sites. Buses run half-hourly between 7.30am and 9pm (services reduce to 9am-6pm Oct-May and hourly 10am-4pm Nov-Apr).

Tickets (€5) can only be purchased on board. Tickets are valid for 24 hours and can be used on all public transport, excluding the airport services.

Suburban buses (blue and white) operate every 15 minutes from 5am to midnight. Tickets (€0.80) are pur-chased at kiosks. Buses from Piraeus to Syntagma (040) and Piraeus to Kifisia (500) run 24 hours.

BIKES

Cycling in Athens is a daring and potentially dangerous pursuit, with no cycle lanes and often reckless drivers. Limit yourself to the pedestrian areas around Thisio and Akropoli and restrict outings to daylight hours. You can hire bikes and go on a variety of group tours through **Acropolis Bikes** (Map p95, E4;

Recommended Modes of Transport

	Syntagma	Acropolis	Plaka & Monastiraki
Syntagma	n/a	metro 2min or walk 15-20min	walk 10-15min or metro 2min
Acropolis	walk 15-20min or metro 2min	n/a	walk 10-15min
Plaka & Monastiraki	walk 10-15min or metro 2min	walk 10-15min	n/a
Gazi – Technopolis	metro 5min	metro 5-10min	metro 5min
National Archaeological Museum	trolleybus 10min or metro 5min	metro 10min or trolleybus 15min	metro 5min
Piraeus	metro 25min	metro 30min	metro 25min
Glyfada	tram 45min or bus 40min	tram 45min or bus 40min	bus 30-40min or tram 40-45min
Kifisia	metro 35min	metro 30min	metro 30min

☎ 210 324 5793; www.acropolisbikes .gr; Aristidou 10-12, Omonia; 4hr rental €10, tours €20-30).

TAXI

Athens' yellow taxis are relatively cheap but hailing one can be incredibly frustrating and the experience a matter of potluck.

During busy times, you'll have to do as the Athenians do and stand on the pavement shouting your destination as they pass (not necessarily slowing down). If a taxi is going your way, the driver may stop even with passengers inside. The fare is not shared – check the meter when you get in, deduct that amount from the final fare and add the flag fall.

Athens' taxi drivers have a terrible reputation for ripping off tourists and while this is not necessarily the norm, exercise caution in case you land one of the nasty ones (beware, it's often the friendly ones who are the worst). Demand to be driven to the police

Gazi – Technopolis	National Archaeological Museum	Piraeus	Glyfada	Kifisia
metro 5min	trolleybus 10min or metro 5min	metro 25min	tram 45min or bus 40min	metro 35min
metro 5-10min	metro 10min or trolleybus 15min	metro 30min	bus 40min or tram 45min	metro 30min
metro 5min	metro 5min	metro 25min	bus 30-40min or tram 40-45min	metro 30-35min
n/a	metro 10min	metro 25min	metro 5min, bus 30-45min or tram 30-45min	metro 30min
metro 10mins	n/a	metro 20min	bus 30-45min or tram 30-45min	metro 30min
metro 25min	metro 20min	n/a	bus 30min or tram 30min	metro 40min
bus 30-40min, metro 5min or tram 40-45min, metro 5min	bus 30-40min or tram 40-45min	bus 30min or tram 30min	n/a	metro 35min or bus 25min or tram 25min
metro 35min	metro 30min	metro 40min	bus 25min or tram 25min or metro 35min	n/a

if you have a dispute or make sure you get a receipt with the driver's details. Despite bans, many drivers continue to smoke in cabs.

Fees should be displayed in the cab and drivers are required to provide a receipt on request.

Flag-fall is €1, with additional surcharges from ports, railway and bus stations (€1) and the airport (€3.20), and for baggage (per item over 10kg €0.32). The €0.32 per kilometre day-tariff increases to €0.60 between midnight and 5am (tariff 2). The minimum fare is €2.80. Most journeys around downtown Athens cost between €2.80 and €4.

You can also call a radio taxi (€2.50 charge).

Enotita (☎ 8011 151 000)
Ikaros (☎ 210 515 2800)
Kosmos (☎ 18300)

PRACTICALITIES
BUSINESS HOURS

Banking hours are from 8am to 2.30pm Monday to Thursday and 8am to 2pm Friday. General shopping hours are 9am to 3pm Monday, Wednesday and Saturday; 9am to 2.30pm and 5.30pm to 8.30pm Tuesday, Thursday and Friday (5pm to 8pm in winter). Most major shopping strips in central Athens, however, are open all day; in Plaka and tourist areas they stay open until

about 11pm. Department stores and supermarkets open 8am to 8pm Monday to Friday and 8am to 6pm Saturday. Central post offices operate 7.30am to 8pm. Restaurants across the city will generally serve lunch between 1pm and 3pm, sometimes even until 4pm, and dinner is served from 9pm until late, though most restaurants in tourist areas stay open all day.

DISCOUNTS

Children under 18 and EU students get free admission to state-run museums and archaeological sites (and some private museums), as do classics and fine-arts students from non-EU countries. Families can also get discounts at some museums and galleries.

Students with an International Student Identity Card (ISIC) should get discounts to archaeological sites, museums, cinemas and public transport.

Card-carrying EU pensioners can claim discounts at museums, cinemas, theatres, ancient sites and on public transport. Others should declare their status, as it is up to the discretion of each institution.

Many museums and archaeological sites have free admission on certain days of the year (see p32 for further details).

ELECTRICITY

The electric current in Athens is 220V, 50Hz, as in the rest of Europe. Plugs are standard continental, with two round pins. USA and Canada use 110V, 60Hz, so it's safest to use a transformer.

EMERGENCIES

Athens has 24-hour dedicated **Visitor Emergency Assistance** (☎ 112 toll-free) in English or French or you can try the **Tourist Police** (☎ 171), who can assist or refer you to the nearest police station.

Ambulance (☎ 166)
Fire (☎ 199)
Police (☎ 100)
SOS Doctors (☎ 1016)

HOLIDAYS

New Year's Day 1 January
Epiphany 6 January
Ash Monday February/March
Greek Independence Day 25 March
Good Friday March/April
Easter Sunday March/April
Labour Day/Spring Festival 1 May
Agiou Pnevmatos June
Feast of the Assumption of the Virgin 15 August
Ohi Day 28 October
Christmas Day 25 December
Agios Stefanos 26 December

INTERNET

There are plenty of internet cafés around town (€3-4 per hour) and most midrange and top-end hotels provide internet access. Free wi-fi hotspots are emerging around town, including the area around Plateia Syntagma, Thisio and Plateia Kotzia, while many cafés offer free wi-fi.

You can buy good value pre-paid dial-up internet cards at OTE (Greece's main telecommunications carrier) shops or Germanos stores if you've got a laptop.
City of Athens (www.cityofathens.gr)
Greek Travel Pages (www.gtp.gr) General tourism information
Lonely Planet (www.lonelyplanet.com) Speedy links to many Greek websites
Ministry of Culture (www.culture.gr) Information on museums, archaeological sites and cultural events

LANGUAGE

The official language is Greek, but many people, particularly the younger generation and those in the tourism sector, speak English, too.

Probably the oldest European language, Greek has an oral tradition dating back some 4000 years and a written tradition of about 3000 years. Modern Greek developed from a number of regional dialects, mainly from the south. Greek has its own distinctive 24-letter alphabet, from which the Cyrillic alphabet was derived. Transliterations into the Roman alphabet are used in this guide; note that the letter combination dh is pronounced as the 'th' in 'them'.

BASICS

Hello.	yia su/yia sas (informal/formal and plural)
Goodbye.	an·*di*·o
How are you?	ti *ka*·nis
Fine. And you?	ka·*la* e·*si*
Excuse me.	sigh·*no*·mi
Yes.	ne
No.	*o*·hi
Thank you.	ef·kha·ri·*sto*
You're welcome (That's fine).	pa·ra·ka·*lo*
Do you speak English?	mi·*la* te ang·gli·*ka*? (formal)
I (don't) understand.	(dhen) ka·ta·la·*ve*·no
How much is it?	*po*·so *ka*·ni?

EATING & DRINKING

That was delicious!	*i*·tan no·sti·*mo*·ta·to!
I'm a vegetarian.	*i*·me hor·to·*fa*·ghos
Please bring the bill.	to lo·ghar·ya·*zmo*, pa·ra·ka·*lo*
I'd like ...	tha *i*·the·la ...
a beer, please	*mi*·a *bi*·ra pa·ra·ka·*lo*

EMERGENCIES

I'm ill.	*i*·me *a*·ro·stos/sti (m/f)
Help!	vo·*i*·thia!
Call ...!	fo·*nak*·ste ...!
a doctor	*e*·na yi·a·*tro*
the police	tin a·sti·no·*mi*·a

DAYS & NUMBERS

When?	*po*·te?
today	*si*·me·ra
tomorrow	*av*·ri·o
yesterday	hthes

0	mi·*dhen*
1	*e*·nas/*mi*·a/*e*·na (m/f/n)
2	*dhi*·o
3	tris (m&f)/*tri*·a (n)
4	*te*·se·ris (m&f)/*te*·se·ra (n)
5	*pen*·de
6	*e*·xi
7	ep·*ta*
8	oh·*to*
9	e·*ne*·a
10	*dhe*·ka
20	*ik*·o·si
30	tri·*an*·da
40	sa·*ran*·da
50	pe·*nin*·da
60	*exin*·da
70	ev·dho·*min*·da
80	oh·*dhon*·da
90	*enenin*da
100	e·ka·*to*
1000	*hi*·li·i/*hi*·li·ez/*hi*·li·a (m/f/n)
2000	*dhi*·o chi·*li*·a·dhez

MONEY

Greece adopted the single EU currency, the euro (pronounced 'evro' in Greek) in 2002.

NEWSPAPERS & MAGAZINES

The biggest selection of foreign-press publications can be found at the 24-hour kiosks in Omonia and Syntagma, and in Plateia Kolonaki.

The main English-language papers are the English edition of *Kathimerini* (www.ekathimerini.com), published daily (except Sunday) with the *International Herald Tribune*, and the weekly *Athens News* (www.athensnews.gr) and newcomer *Athens Plus*, published by *Kathimerini*. Both publish movie and entertainment listings.

Magazines include the monthly city magazine *Insider* and bimonthly *Odyssey* diaspora magazine. The weekly *Athinorama*, *Athens Voice* and *Lifo* free press are the best source of information about events in the city if you can read Greek.

ORGANISED TOURS

Sights in Athens are easy to get to on your own so the only real advantage of standard Athens sightseeing bus tours (€52) is the guide. With the exception of key sites, many are drive-by tours, so check details. Tours can be booked through hotels or travel agencies (half-day tours from €40; day trips €80 to €90). Many companies offer tailored tours or special interest tours.

BUS TOURS

Chat (Map pp40–1, E4; ☎ 210 323 0827; www.chatours.gr; Xenofontos 9, Syntagma; ☼ 9am-7.30pm Mon-Sat) City sights and excursions.

Hop In Sightseeing (Map p51, D4; ☎ 210 428 5500; www.hopin.com; Leoforos Syngrou 19, Makrygianni; ☼ 6am-10pm) Allows you to get on and off the bus over two days (also does hotel pick-ups).

Key Tours (Map p123, A6; ☎ 210 923 3166; www.keytours.gr; Kaliroïs 4, Mets)

ARCHAEOLOGICAL TOURS

Athenian Days (☎ 210 864 0415, 6977660798; www.atheniandays.co.uk) Classicist Andrew Farrington leads private tailor-made cultural and historical introductions to the city for groups up to six. Pre-booking essential.

Panhellenic Guides Federation (☎ 210 322 9705; Apollonos 9a) Can arrange private tours of archaeological sites by accredited guides (four hours about €90).

Rania Vassiliadou (☎ 210 940 3932; raniavassiliadou.virtualave.net) Provides a well-regarded service around Athens' archaeological sites and day trips further afield for up to six people.

ALTERNATIVE TOURS

City Walking Tours (☎ 210 884 7269; www.athenswalkingtours.gr) Offers several walks around the city from the markets to the archaeological sites (€29).

Scoutway (Map p123, A3; ☎ 210 729 9111; www.scoutway.gr; Ptolemeon 1, Pangrati) Scoutway runs a range of innovative interactive tours and day trips, from Athens nightlife, an ancient Greece theme walk, hikes, mountain biking to the ancient mines at Lavrio and bungee jumping on the Corinth Canal.

Trekking Hellas (Map pp40–1, F5; ☎ 210 331 0323; www.outdoorsgreece.com; Filellinon 7, Plaka) Runs various activities from an Athens walking tour (€37) to culinary theme walks.

ISLAND TOURS

Many visitors can't resist a day trip to a nearby island. Pricey day cruises to Hydra (p150), Poros and Aegina usually include a buffet lunch and onboard entertainment with traditional dancing (around €95; enquire at Chat or Hop In Sightseeing, p189) but you're probably better off doing it on your own.

TELEPHONE

Greece uses the same GSM system as most EU countries, Asia and Australia. You can buy local prepaid mobile phone cards (that give you a Greek number) at kiosks. See also the inside front cover of this guide.

COUNTRY & CITY CODES

Athens (☎ 210)
Greece (☎ 30)
International access code (☎ 00)

USEFUL PHONE NUMBERS

Duty hospitals/pharmacies (☎ 1434)
International directory and operator (☎ 161)
Local directory inquiries (☎ 11888)
Reverse charge (collect) calls (☎ 161)

TIPPING

Tipping is customary but not compulsory. In restaurants, the service charge is included in the bill, but most people still leave a small tip or at least round up the bill. This applies to taxis as well (if they haven't already added it) – a small tip for good service is appreciated.

TOURIST INFORMATION

The **Greek National Tourism Organisation** (GNTO; Map pp40-1, F4; ☎ 210 331 0392; www.gnto.gr; Leoforos Vasilissis Amalias 26a, Syntagma; ☉ 9am-7pm Mon-Fri, 10am-4pm Sat & Sun) referred to as EOT (Ellinikos Organismos Tourismou), has tourist information offices in Athens and at the airport.

Helpful multilingual staff provide a handy free map of Athens, public transport information and brochures. You can also pick up a free copy of the glossy *Athens & Attica* booklet.
GNTO airport branch (☎ 210 353 0445; arrivals hall; ☉ 9am-7pm Mon-Fri, 10am-4pm Sat & Sun)
Tourist police (☎ 171; ☉ 24hr)

TRAVELLERS WITH DISABILITIES

Facilities for the mobility impaired are a recent and relatively rare phenomenon in Greece. Most public buildings and major museums are now wheelchair-friendly and a special lift allows access to parts of the Acropolis. Many hotels have upgraded their facilities in the lead up to the 2004 Paralympics, the metro has lifts and the airport has excellent facilities.

But making the rest of the city accessible is a monumental challenge. Many museums and older buildings have stairs, most archaeological sites are not wheelchair friendly, public transport can be crowded and restaurants often have toilets downstairs.

Newer buses and trolleybuses are wider and have seats assigned for those with disabilities, but getting on or off isn't easy.

For more information, contact the **Panhellenic Union of Paraplegic & Physically Challenged** (☎ 210 483 2564; www.pasipka.gr; Dimitsanis 3-5, Moschato).

>INDEX

See also separate subindexes for See (p195), Shop (p197), Eat (p198), Drink (p199) and Play (p199).

000 map pages

000 **map pages**

INDEX

000 map pages